Modern Critical Interpretations

Henry James's
The Portrait of a Lady

Modern Critical Interpretations

These and other titles in preparation

Modern Critical Interpretations

Henry James's
The Portrait of a Lady

Edited and with an introduction by
Harold Bloom
Sterling Professor of the Humanities
Yale University

Chelsea House Publishers
NEW YORK ◇ PHILADELPHIA

© 1987 by Chelsea House Publishers, a division
of Main Line Book Co.

Introduction © 1987 by Harold Bloom

Printed and bound in the United States of America

10 9 8 7 6 5 4 3 2

∞ The paper used in this publication meets the minimum
requirements of the American National Standard for
Permanence of Paper for Printed Library Materials,
Z39.48-1984.

Library of Congress Cataloging-in-Publication Data
Henry James's The portrait of a lady.
   (Modern critical interpretations)
   Bibliography: p.
   Includes index.
   1. James, Henry, 1843–1916. Portrait of a lady.
I. Bloom, Harold.   II. Series.
PS2116.P63H46   1987   813'.4   86-24438
ISBN 1-55546-008-9

Contents

Editor's Note

This book brings together what I regard as the best criticism yet devoted to Henry James's masterwork, *The Portrait of a Lady*. The critical essays are reprinted here in the chronological order of their original publication. I am grateful to Daniel Klotz for his assistance in research upon this volume.

My introduction first considers the relation of James to Emerson, and then analyzes Isabel Archer as a heroine of Emersonian Self-Reliance. Richard Poirier begins the chronological sequence of criticism with a subtle portrait of James's high mode of comedy, which can portray Isabel's march to ruin without demeaning her exquisite sense of human possibility.

Laurence Bedwell Holland, in perhaps the most thorough study ever given us of the novel, usefully emphasizes the *Portrait's* relation to Hawthorne's *Scarlet Letter,* its undoubted precursor. In Nina Baym's essay, the 1881 edition is demonstrated to have been, in some crucial ways, more interesting than the 1908 revision. Elizabeth Allen, dwelling upon Isabel's inheritance, brings us a telling emphasis upon Pansy, who represents woman as object.

For David M. Lubin, the portrait of Isabel is really James's self-portrait, a judgment that serves as prelude to the two extraordinary essays in criticism that conclude this book. In the first, the distinguished Portuguese critic Maria Irene Ramalho de Sousa Santos reads the novel more as tragedy than as comedy, in an elegant contrast to Poirier's strong interpretation. For Ramalho de Sousa Santos, Isabel confers a tragic dimension upon herself through her conquest of freedom by the hard return to Rome, and to Osmond. Deborah Esch, in the final essay, subjects the novel to the most acute and advanced rhetorical analysis it has received. If Esch is correct, then "freedom for Isabel is above all freedom to forget," which is an ironic or allegorical reading of her Emersonian Self-Reliance, with its drive against history.

Introduction

I

The intense critical admirers of Henry James go so far as to call him the major American writer, or even the most accomplished novelist in the English language. The first assertion neglects only Walt Whitman, while the second partly evades the marvelous sequence that moves from Samuel Richardson's *Clarissa* through Jane Austen on to George Eliot, and the alternative tradition that goes from Fielding through Dickens to Joyce. James is certainly the crucial American novelist, and in his best works the true peer of Austen and George Eliot. His precursor, Hawthorne, is more than fulfilled in the splendors of *The Portrait of a Lady* and *The Wings of the Dove,* giant descendants of *The Marble Faun,* while the rival American novelists—Melville, Twain, Dreiser, Faulkner—survive comparison with James only by being so totally unlike him. Unlikeness makes Faulkner— particularly in his great phase—a true if momentary rival, and perhaps if you are to find a non-Jamesian sense of sustained power in the American novel, you need to seek out our curious antithetical tradition that moves between *Moby-Dick* and its darker descendants: *As I Lay Dying, Miss Lonelyhearts, The Crying of Lot 49.* The normative consciousness of our prose fiction, first prophesied by *The Scarlet Letter,* was forged by Henry James, whose spirit lingers not only in palpable disciples like Edith Wharton in *The Age of Innocence* and Willa Cather in her superb *A Lost Lady,* but more subtly (because merged with Joseph Conrad's aura) in novelists as various as Fitzgerald, Hemingway, and Warren. It seems clear that the relation of James to American prose fiction is precisely analogous to Whitman's relation to our poetry; each is, in his own sphere, what Emerson prophesied as the Central Man who would come and change all things forever, in a celebration of the American Newness.

The irony of James's central position among our novelists is palpable, since, like the much smaller figure of T. S. Eliot later on, James abandoned his nation and eventually became a British subject, after having been born a citizen in Emerson's America. But it is a useful commonplace of criticism that James remained the most American of novelists, not less peculiarly nationalistic in *The Ambassadors* than he had been in *Daisy Miller* and *The American*. James, a subtle if at times perverse literary critic, understood very well what we continue to learn and relearn; an American writer can be Emersonian or anti-Emersonian, but even a negative stance towards Emerson always leads back again to his formulation of the post-Christian American religion of *Self*-Reliance. Overt Emersonians like Thoreau, Whitman, and Frost are no more pervaded by the Sage of Concord than are anti-Emersonians like Hawthorne, Melville, and Eliot. Perhaps the most haunted are those writers who evade Emerson, yet never leave his dialectical ambiance, a group that includes Emily Dickinson, Henry James, and Wallace Stevens.

Emerson was for Henry James something of a family tradition, though that in itself hardly accounts for the plain failure of very nearly everything that the novelist wrote about the essayist. James invariably resorts to a tone of ironic indulgence on the subject of Emerson, which is hardly appropriate to the American prophet of Power, Fate, Illusion, and Wealth. I suggest that James unknowingly mixed Emerson up with the sage's good friend Henry James, Sr., whom we dismiss as a Swedenborgian, but who might better be characterized as an American Gnostic speculator, in Emerson's mode, though closer in eminence to, say, Bronson Alcott, than to the author of *The Conduct of Life*.

The sane and sacred Emerson was a master of evasions, particularly when disciples became too pressing, whether upon personal or spiritual matters. The senior Henry James is remembered now for having fathered Henry, William, and Alice, and also for his famous outburst against Emerson, whom he admired on the other side of idolatry: "O you man without a handle!"

The junior Henry James, overtly celebrating Emerson, nevertheless remarked: "It is hardly too much, or too little, to say of Emerson's writings in general that they were not composed at all." "Composed" is the crucial word there, and makes me remember a beautiful moment in Stevens's "The Poems of our Climate":

> There would still remain the never-resting mind,
> So that one would want to escape, come back
> To what had been so long composed.

Emerson's mind, never merely restless, indeed was never-resting, as was the mind of every member of the James family. The writings of Emerson, not composed at all, constantly come back to what had been so long composed, to what his admirer Nietzsche called the primordial poem of mankind, the fiction that we have knocked together and called our cosmos. James was far too subtle not to have known this. He chose not to know it, because he needed a provincial Emerson even as he needed a provincial Hawthorne, just as he needed a New England that never was: simple, gentle, and isolated, even a little childlike.

The days when T. S. Eliot could wonder why Henry James had not carved up R. W. Emerson seem safely past, but we ought to remember Eliot's odd complaint about James as critic: "Even in handling men whom he could, one supposes, have carved joint from joint—Emerson or Norton—his touch is uncertain; there is a desire to be generous, a political motive, an admission (in dealing with American writers) that under the circumstances this was the best possible, or that it has fine qualities." Aside from appearing to rank Emerson with Charles Eliot Norton (which is comparable to ranking Freud with Bernard Berenson), this unamiable judgment reduces Emerson, who was and is merely the mind of America, to the stature of a figure who might, at most, warrant the condescension of James (and of Eliot). The cultural polemic involved is obvious, and indeed obsessive, in Eliot, but though pleasanter in James is really no more acceptable:

Of the three periods into which his life divides itself, the first was (as in the case of most men) that of movement, experiment and selection—that of effort too and painful probation. Emerson had his message, but he was a good while looking for his form— the form which, as he himself would have said, he never completely found and of which it was rather characteristic of him that his later years (with their growing refusal to give him the *word*), wishing to attack him in his most vulnerable point, where his tenure was least complete, had in some degree the effect of despoiling him. It all sounds rather bare and stern, Mr. Cabot's account of his youth and early manhood, and we get an impression of a terrible paucity of alternatives. If he would be neither a farmer nor a trader he could "teach school"; that was the main resource and a part of the general educative process of the young New Englander who proposed to devote himself to the things of the mind. There was an advantage in the nudity, however, which was that, in Emerson's case at least, the things of the mind did get themselves admirably well considered. If it be his great distinction and his special sign that he had a more vivid conception of the moral life than any one else, it is probably not fanciful to say that he owed it in part to the limited way in which he saw our capacity for living illustrated. The plain, God-fearing, practical society which surrounded him was not fertile in variations: it had great intelligence and energy, but it moved altogether in the straightforward direction. On three occasions later—three journeys to Europe—he was introduced to a more complicated world; but his spirit, his moral taste, as it were, abode always within the undecorated walls of his youth. There he could dwell with that ripe unconsciousness of evil which is one of the most beautiful signs by which we know him. His early writings are full of quaint animadversion upon the vices of the place and time, but there is something charmingly vague, light and general in the arraignment. Almost the worst he can say is that these vices are negative and that his fellow-townsmen are not heroic. We feel that his first impressions were gathered in a community from which misery and extravagance, and either extreme, of any sort, were equally absent. What the life of New England fifty years ago offered to the observer was the common lot, in a kind of achromatic picture, without particular intensifications. It was from this table of the usual, the merely typical joys and sorrows that he proceeded to generalise—a fact that accounts in some degree for a certain inadequacy and thinness in his enumerations. But it helps to account also for his direct, intimate vision of the soul itself—not in its emotions, its contortions and perversions, but in its passive, exposed, yet healthy form. He knows the nature of man and the long tradition of its dangers; but we feel that whereas he can put his finger on the remedies, lying for the most part, as they do, in the deep recesses of virtue, of the spirit, he has only a kind of hearsay, uninformed acquaintance with the disorders. It would require some ingenuity, the reader may say too much, to trace closely this correspondence between his genius and the frugal, dutiful, happy but decidedly lean Boston of the past, where there was a great deal of will but very little fulcrum—like a ministry without an opposition.

The genius itself it seems to me impossible to contest—I mean the genius for seeing character as a real and supreme thing. Other writers have arrived at a more complete expression: Wordsworth and Goethe, for instance, give one a sense of having found their form, whereas with Emerson we never lose the sense that he is still seeking it. But no one has had so steady and constant, and above all so natural, a vision of what we require and what we are capable of in the way of aspiration and independence. With Emerson it is ever the special capacity for moral experience—always that and only that. We have the impression, somehow, that life had never bribed him to look at anything but the soul; and indeed in the world in which he grew up and lived the bribes and lures, and beguilements and prizes, were few. He was in an admirable position for showing, what he constantly endeavoured to show, that the prize was within. Any one who in New England at that time could do that was sure of success, of listeners and sympathy: most of all, of course, when it was a question of doing it with such a divine persuasiveness. Moreover, the way in which Emerson did it added to the charm—by word of mouth, face to face, with a rare, irresistible voice and a beautiful mild, modest authority. If Mr. Arnold is struck with the limited degree in which he was a man of letters I suppose it is because he is more struck with his having been, as it were, a man of lectures. But the lecture surely was never more purged of its grossness—the quality in it that suggests a strong light and a big brush—than as it issued from Emerson's lips; so far from being a vulgarisation, it was simply the esoteric made audible, and instead of treating the few as the many, after the usual fashion of gentlemen on platforms, he treated the many as the few. There was probably no other society at that time in which he would have got so many persons to understand that; for we think the better of his audience as we read him, and wonder where else people would have had so much moral attention to give. It is to be remembered however that during the winter of 1847–48, on the occasion of his second visit to England, he found many listeners in London and in provincial cities. Mr. Cabot's volumes are full of evidence of the satisfactions he offered, the delights and revelations he may be said to have promised, to a race which had to seek its entertainment, its rewards and consolations, almost exclusively in the moral world. But his own writings are fuller still; we find an instance almost wherever we open them.

It is astonishing to me that James judged Emerson's "great distinction" and "special sign" to be "that he had a more vivid conception of the moral life than any one else," unless "the moral life" has an altogether Jamesian meaning. I would rather say that the great distinction and the special sign of James's fiction is that it represents a more vivid conception of the moral life than even Jane Austen or George Eliot could convey to us. Emerson is not much more concerned with morals than he is with manners; his subjects are power, freedom, and fate. As for "that ripe unconsciousness of evil" that James found in Emerson, I have not been able to find it myself, after reading Emerson almost daily for the last twenty years, and I am reminded of Yeats's late essay on Shelley's *Prometheus Unbound,* in which Yeats declares that his skeptical and passionate precursor, great poet that he certainly was, necessarily lacked the Vision of Evil. The necessity in both strong misreadings, James's and Yeats's, was to clear more space for themselves.

Jealous as I am for Emerson, I can recognize that no critic has matched James in seeing and saying what Emerson's strongest virtue is: "But no one has had so steady and constant, and above all so natural, a vision of what we require and what we are capable of in the way of aspiration and independence." No one, that is, except Henry James, for that surely is the quest of Isabel Archer towards her own quite Emersonian vision of aspiration and independence. "The moral world" is James's phrase and James's emphasis. Emerson's own emphasis, I suspect, was considerably more pragmatic than that of James. When James returned to America in 1904 on a visit, after twenty years of self-exile, he went back to Concord and recorded his impressions in *The American Scene:*

> It is odd, and it is also exquisite, that these witnessing ways should be the last ground on which we feel moved to ponderation of the "Concord school"—to use, I admit, a futile expression; or rather, I should doubtless say, it *would* be odd if there were not inevitably something absolute in the fact of Emerson's all but lifelong connection with them. We may smile a little as we "drag in" Weimar, but I confess myself, for my part, much more satisfied than not by our happy equivalent, "in American money," for Goethe and Schiller. The money is a potful in the second case as in the first, and if Goethe, in the one, represents the gold and Schiller the silver, I find (and quite putting aside any bimetallic prejudice) the same good relation in the other between Emerson and Thoreau. I open Emerson for the same benefit for which I open Goethe, the sense of moving in large

intellectual space, and that of the gush, here and there, out of the rock, of the crystalline cupful, in wisdom and poetry, in Wahrheit and Dichtung; and whatever I open Thoreau for (I needn't take space here for the good reasons) I open him oftener than I open Schiller. Which comes back to our feeling that the rarity of Emerson's genius, which has made him so, for the attentive peoples, the first, and the one really rare, American spirit in letters, couldn't have spent his career in a charming woody, watery place, for so long socially and typically and, above all, interestingly homogeneous, without an effect as of the communication to it of something ineffaceable. It was during his long span his immediate concrete, sufficient world; it gave him his nearest vision of life, and he drew half his images, we recognize, from the revolution of its seasons and the play of its manners. I don't speak of the other half, which he drew from elsewhere. It is admirably, to-day, as if we were still seeing these things *in* those images, which stir the air like birds, dim in the eventide, coming home to nest. If one had reached a "time of life" one had thereby at least heard him lecture; and not a russet leaf fell for me, while I was there, but fell with an Emersonian drop.

That is a beautiful study of the nostalgias and tells us, *contra* T. S. Eliot, what James's relation to Emerson actually was. We know how much that is essential in William James was quarried out of Emerson, particularly from the essay "Experience," which gave birth to Pragmatism. Henry James was not less indebted to Emerson than William James was. *The Portrait of a Lady* is hardly an Emersonian novel; perhaps *The Scarlet Letter* actually is closer to that. Yet Isabel Archer is Emerson's daughter, just as Lambert Strether is Emerson's heir. The Emersonian aura also lingers on even in the ghostly tales of Henry James.

II

Isabel Archer may be the fictional heroine above all others with whom modern literary intellectuals are certain to fall in love. That sounds funny, yet is intended quite seriously. That Henry James himself was in love with her is palpable. Critics and biographers frequently associate her with Minny Temple, James's beloved cousin, who had died at the age of twenty-four. That James was deeply in love with Minny Temple we may doubt, but if he ever was in love with any woman, it was with her, and with her representation in the heroine of *The Portrait of a Lady.*

Leon Edel makes the interesting (and disquieting) suggestion that Isabel is a portrait not only of Minny but of James himself:

> The allusion to her "flame-like spirit" suggests that Isabel is an image of James's long-dead cousin Minny Temple, whom he would describe in the same way. But if Isabel, with her eager imagination and intellectual shortcomings, has something of Minny in her make-up, she has much of Henry himself. He endows her with the background of his own Albany childhood, and when he sends her to Europe and makes her into an heiress, he places her in a predicament similar to his own. James was hardly an "heir"; but his pen had won him a measure of the freedom which others possess through wealth. In posing the questions: what would Isabel do with her new-found privileges? where would she turn? how behave? he was seeking answers to the transcendentalism of Concord: his novel is a critique of American "self-reliance."

A much more sophisticated analysis of the problematical ways in which James's masterpiece is a critique of Emerson is provided by Richard Poirier in his *The Comic Sense of Henry James* (1960):

> This connection between James and Emerson is worth attention because . . . the idealistic and romantic attitudes towards experience which are to be found in Emerson's essays are observable as well in the whole body of significant American fiction from Melville and Hawthorne to Faulkner. The relationship between James and Emerson is important within the larger fact that both of them subscribe to attitudes which are discernibly American, regardless of whether the literature derives from New England, New York, the South, or the West. It has often been said that Isabel Archer is an imitation of George Eliot's Dorothea Brooke, but it is apparent from all the novels of James which have no resemblance to *Middlemarch,* and from their Emersonian echoes, that *The Portrait of a Lady* could have brought the theme of aspiration to the point it does without the help of George Eliot.

Poirier's important formulation seems to me the necessary beginning of critical wisdom concerning *The Portrait of a Lady.* As Poirier observes, the novel's severest irony "is the degree to which Osmond is a mock version of the transcendentalist," which makes it not surprising that "Isabel, whose mental processes are authentically Emersonian, should see an image of herself in the man she marries." I would add to Poirier's point that Osmond is as much a mock version of the Paterian aesthete as he is of the Emersonian transcendentalist, which is again appropriate, since Isabel is both an authentic Emersonian and a true Paterian consciousness. Her blindness as to Osmond's true nature, a blindness not cleared away until too late, may be taken as James's implicit judgment that Emerson and Pater alike had no true vision of evil, but that would make James too much a forerunner of T. S. Eliot and too little an heir of George Eliot, to whom his affinities are far more profound. It makes little sense to say that Dorothea Brooke in *Middlemarch* falls into her initial dreadful marriage because her Wordsworthian idealism cannot accommodate reality, and even less sense to believe that Isabel Archer is a victim either of Emersonian aspiration or of Paterian sensibility.

Whatever James took Emersonian self-reliance to be, we can recognize in Isabel her own version of Emerson's post-Christian American religion, with its grand style of aspiration, that seems to center for James's Lady in the Sage of Concord's most dangerous admonition:

> Life only avails, not the having lived. Power ceases in the instant
> of repose; it resides in the moment of transition from a past to
> a new state, in the shooting of the gulf, in the darting to an aim.
> ("Self-Reliance")

Isabel declines to be one of the secondary women, which means that she rejects European history. As a believer in self-reliance, she quests after a knowing in which she herself will be known. Does her quest fail as massively as the disaster of her marriage to Osmond would seem to indicate? Poirier, reading the novel as Jamesian comedy, gives a complex answer, which informs me without altogether persuading me. Is Isabel's what Emerson called a great defeat, necessarily unacceptable to Americans because we demand victory? Is James somehow more Virgilian than Emersonian? In Poirier's judgment, as I interpret it, James is both, because Isabel ends as that sublimely unlikely compound ghost, a Virgilian Emersonian:

> James had a very tenuous and unorganized sense of the connec-
> tion between sexual psychology, on the one hand, and, on the
> other, the desire for freedom and death. He had a very clear and
> conscious idea, however, about the relationship between free-

dom and death, and it is that which comes through to us from the final chapters. What Caspar offers her in the garden is an old call to action and freedom: "The world is all before us." While the intensity of her reaction to Caspar deserves the closest attention, the reasons for her refusal to go away with him need no explanation. She is simply not deeply enough in love with him nor has she ever been. When she hurries away from him, however, she is also escaping his call to leave the "garden" of her dreams now that, like Eden after the fall, it has become a place of desolation. The Miltonic echo in his plea is unmistakably placed there. The same line occurs much earlier in the novel when Isabel sees her relatives off for America. Having done her duty by these figures out of her past, and in possession of what seems unhampered independence, she walks away from the station into the London fog: "The world lay all before her—she could do whatever she chose." In James's use of the phraseology of *Paradise Lost* ("The world lay all before them, where to choose / Their place of rest"), there is not only a Miltonic sadness, but also an irony derived from the fact that neither Isabel nor Caspar is free to choose anything. His life is in useless bondage to his love for her, while hers is dedicated to its errors. And there is nothing in her act which holds the promise, as does Adam and Eve's, of eventual happiness through suffering, even though Ralph assures her that there is. Her action is absolutely within the logic of her Emersonian idealism, so much so that the logic takes its vengeance. In effect she tells the reader, to borrow from "The Transcendentalist," that "you think me the child of my circumstances: I make my circumstance,"—including, one might add, "my own misery." It is of no importance to her that, in fact, she has been so calculatingly deceived by other people that it is preposterous to assume all the responsibility for her own past. To admit this would be finally to subscribe to Madame Merle's view that the "self" is determined, in part, by "an envelope of circumstances" that one does not always create. Isabel's action at the end is fully consistent with everything she does earlier. Now, however, she asserts her idealism of self not in innocence but in full knowledge of the world. For that reason, freedom, which was the condition of self-creation, becomes a form of indifference to the fact that returning to Rome will, as Caspar admonishes, cost her her life.

The overt anti-Emersonianism of Madame Merle's view of the self, noted both by Philip Rahv and by Poirier, seems to me an involuntary or repressed allusion on James's part. Yet I read the novel's conclusion a touch more hopefully than Poirier does. Caspar Goodwood is hardly the answer, any more than Warburton was, and James himself labored to make certain that Ralph Touchett could not be the answer either. Since Isabel fuses Minny Temple and James himself, no marriage could be the answer, and the male otherness of Goodwood only drives Isabel back to the house of death. When James revised the novel for the New York edition, his emphasis upon both Isabel's possibilities for freedom and the severe limitations set by context and fate upon that freedom became obsessive, particularly in regard to Isabel's hovering dread of the erotic threat to her inward liberty. The "disagreeably strong push, a kind of hardness of presence, in his way of rising before her," clearly dismisses the revised Goodwood as a distasteful phallic phenomenon, and so unacceptable to Isabel, who finds, however absurdly, in the repellant Osmond "a future at a high level of consciousness of the beautiful." Anthony J. Mazzella, in his close study of the novel's revisions, finds in "the new Isabel" a more remarkable consciousness, both of freedom and of vulnerability, than was possessed by the original Isabel. This is surely equivalent to the difference between the Emerson of "Self-Reliance" and the dark necessitarian of *The Conduct of Life,* so that we move from the sage who insisted that "the only sin is limitation" to the theoretician of "Power" who warns us that "nothing is got for nothing," and that this is the true law of Compensation.

It cannot be accidental that Isabel's psychosexual vulnerabilities are so like James's own (as far as we are able to tell) and that her apotropaic gestures are essentially his also. Leon Edel wisely avoids any overt characterization of the Master's ineluctable modalities of sexual evasiveness, which have been speculated on so bizarrely by others, with suppositions as remarkable as Hemingway's, who jauntily persuaded Scott Fitzgerald that their greatest American precursor had been physically impotent. In *The Sun Also Rises,* the castrating wound of Jake Barnes is related to James's catastrophe, fantasied both as a bicycle and a horse riding accident. Crazy as this was, it is no weirder than the notion even Edel plays with, which is that Henry James never could resolve his homoerotic attachment to his brother William, scarcely less eminent as philosopher and psychologist than Henry was as a novelist.

I suspect that Henry James in his psychosexual orientation resembled Walt Whitman more strongly than he did anyone else in literary history. Like Whitman, his desires were essentially homoerotic, and again like Whitman he appears to have evaded any merely actual fulfillment of those desires. The distrust of human sexuality in both writers is immense, though the truly esoteric and hermetic Whitman proclaimed his ostensible passions for men, women, the soul, and the United States in a deliberately misleading sexual rhetoric, while the oddly less esoteric Master subtly swerved away from any explicitly sexual diction. A close reader of *Song of Myself* comes to realize that Whitman's poetry, and perhaps Whitman himself, was auto-erotic, while the student of James eventually knows that James and his fiction seem to lack the "narcissistic scar" that Freud saw as marking all of us, being a memento of our first failure in love, the loss of our parent of the sex opposite to ours to our parent of the same sex as ours. Whatever his authentic relation to George Eliot and to Trollope, to Hawthorne and to Emerson, James also seems not to have needed to restitute a wounded narcissism as an author. His striking originality as a novelist, nearly akin to Whitman's as a poet, has a still obscure but vital relation to his warding-off of mere sexuality. Just as Whitman is an erotic rather than a sexual poet, since he crosses sex with death, so James is an intensely erotic novelist, while largely eschewing direct representations of the sexual.

Isabel's eros, being transcendental, is not crucified by the failure of her marriage, since her Jamesian desire remains for her own aspiring self and not for any outward companion. Moral readings of *The Portrait of a Lady* seem to me always to fail, because inherited systems of morality— Christian or humanistic—are irrelevant to Isabel's Emersonian self, as they are to Whitman and to James. Distinguished readers always go wrong on this. I think of the novelist Graham Greene, who remarked that James's ruling passion, in the *Portrait* as elsewhere, was the idea of treachery, or the moral philosopher Dorothea Krook, who criticizes Isabel for "fatal aestheticism." Madame Merle's treachery, though it has its interest, remains peripheral to Isabel's fate, and James himself is far more tainted with a "fatal aestheticism" than Isabel or Emerson are. Searching for a tragic flaw in Isabel always leads to the banal discovery that, like Emerson, she supposedly lacks that grand New-Critical, neo-Christian, T. S. Eliotic virtue—a Vision of Evil. But Isabel is the heroine of the American, post-Christian version of the Protestant will; she is the heiress of all the ages, and so inherits from the great sequence of Clarissa Harlowe, Elizabeth Bennet, Emma Woodhouse, and Dorothea Brooke. What matters is the integrity of her will. For her, love entails her conferring of esteem upon others, and accepting back from them only her own authentic self-esteem. Her will declines the Freudian cosmos of mourning and melancholia. No shadow of the object can fall upon her ego. Consider the great scene between her and Goodwood, a scene more visionary than melodramatic, that effectively ends the inward aspect of the novel. Goodwood has echoed Milton: "The world's all before us—and the world's very big," a truth that Isabel knows better than does her perpetually frustrated suitor:

Isabel gave a long murmur, like a creature in pain; it was as if he were pressing something that hurt her. "The world's very small," she said at random; she had an immense desire to appear to resist. She said it at random, to hear herself say something; but it was not what she meant. The world, in truth, had never seemed so large; it seemed to open out, all round her, to take the form of a mighty sea, where she floated in fathomless waters. She had wanted help, and here was help; it had come in a rushing torrent. I know not whether she believed everything he said; but she believed just then that to let him take her in his arms would be the next best thing to her dying. This belief, for a moment, was a kind of rapture, in which she felt herself sink and sink. In the movement she seemed to beat with her feet, in order to catch herself, to feel something to rest on.

"Ah, be mine as I'm yours!" she heard her companion cry. He had suddenly given up argument, and his voice seemed to come, harsh and terrible, through a confusion of vaguer sounds.

This however, of course, was but a subjective fact, as the metaphysicians say; the confusion, the noise of waters, all the rest of it, were in her own swimming head. In an instant she became aware of this. "Do me the greatest kindness of all," she panted. "I beseech you to go away!"

"Ah, don't say that. Don't kill me!" he cried.

She clasped her hands; her eyes were streaming with tears. "As you love me, as you pity me, leave me alone!"

He glared at her a moment through the dusk, and the next instant she felt his arms about her and his lips on her own lips. His kiss was like white lightning, a flash that spread, and spread again, and stayed; and it was extraordinarily as if, while she took it, she felt each thing in his hard manhood that had least pleased her, each aggressive fact of his face, his figure, his presence, justified of its intense identity and made one with this act of possession. So had she heard of those wrecked and under water following a train of images before they sink. But when darkness returned she was free. She never looked about her; she only darted from the spot. There were lights in the windows of the house; they shone far across the lawn. In an extraordinarily short time—for the distance was considerable—she had moved through the darkness (for she saw nothing) and reached the door. Here only she paused. She looked all about her; she listened a little; then she put her hand on the latch. She had not known where to turn; but she knew now. There was a very straight path.

What Isabel's straight path will lead her to is the renewed Emersonian realization that she herself is her own alternative. More than the noise of waters is in her own swimming head. The erotic imagery of this superb encounter is oceanic, but more in the mode of Whitman's maternal, deathly ocean than in what Freud deprecated as "the oceanic sense" of mystical illusion. A mighty sea, fathomless waters, a rushing torrent, and most of all, those wrecked and under water following a train of images before they sink—these figures can be read from at least two radically different perspectives, both Whitmanian enough. One would oppose the waters to Isabel as the eros of otherness that she rejects, but the other would offer the waters as emblem of a world centered upon Isabel, in evidence that she had made her circumstances, and so chose to accept them, the world of Wallace Stevens's "Tea at the Palaz of Hoon":

What was the sea whose tide swept through me there?

Out of my mind the golden ointment rained,
And my ears made the blowing hymns they heard.
I was myself the compass of that sea:

I was the world in which I walked, and what I saw
Or heard or felt came not but from myself;
And there I found myself more truly and more strange.

This is a hymn of self-reliance, and the chanter could be Whitman, or Emerson, or Pater (adding strangeness to beauty in quest of the Romantic). Or she could be Isabel Archer, not at the close of the novel, but beyond, in that resumed difficult marriage with Osmond, whom she no longer loves, and who no longer loves her. But she herself will be the compass of that sea.

Setting the Scene: The Drama and Comedy of Judgment

Richard Poirier

Of all the early novels, *The Portrait of a Lady* offers the fullest expression, both in the relationships among its characters and in the features of its style and composition, of the drama and comedy of judgment. The major artistic problem of the early novels is, at the same time, their subject: the relationship between judgment and pleasure, between knowledge and entertainment, between the limitations or fixities which awareness imposes upon our experience of the world and the freedom of response and aspiration which innocence allows. Isabel Archer, more than any character in James, is an embodiment of these problems, and it is through her that *The Portrait of a Lady* dramatizes a fictional version of them. Since they are also James's problems as a novelist, in his relationship to his reader and to his characters, Isabel's career can be viewed as an enactment of the very concerns which James feels in the process of creating her. Isabel's ambition is James's achievement, and the position she desires from which to see life most knowledgeably and compassionately is, by the testimony of the novel itself, the one which James has attained.

By making Isabel Archer susceptible to his own desire to take an abundantly large and imaginative view of human experience, James involves her in the quest for that personal condition to which all his favourite characters aspire, the condition of freedom. The term "freedom" is very recurrent and important both in James's fiction and in his essays. It defines an ideal to which such characters as Isabel are dedicated, and the condition

From *The Comic Sense of Henry James, A Study of the Early Novels.* © 1960 by Richard Poirier. Oxford University Press, 1960.

within which the great practitioners of James's art have laboured. When he speaks of the world as the subject of the novelist's attention, it is often in language noticeably similar to Isabel's when she is theorizing about her repeated ambition to take "a large human view of her opportunities and obligations," and to the language of others, like Ralph and James, the narrator, who find in her aspirations an incentive to imaginative free-play of their own. In his letter to the Deerfield Summer School in 1889, for example, replying to an invitation to discuss the art of the novel, James gives some advice to the students which has a familiar ring. His letter is an appeal for freedom of observation, for putting aside all meanness and limitation of view. It might well remind us of Ralph's idea of giving Isabel, through a fortune, the freedom to take full advantage of her desire "to begin by getting a general impression of life":

> "Oh, do something from your point of view; an ounce of example is worth a ton of generalities; do something with the great art and the great form; do something with life. You each have an impression colored by your individual conditions; make that into a picture, a picture framed by your own personal wisdom, your glimpse of the American world. The field is vast for freedom, for study, for observation, for satire, for truth. . . . I have only two little words for the matter remotely approaching to rule or doctrine; one is life and the other freedom. Tell the ladies and gentlemen, the ingenious inquirers, to consider life directly and closely, and not to be put off with mean and puerile falsities, and be conscientious about it. It is infinitely large, various and comprehensive. Every sort of mind will find what it looks for in it, whereby the novel becomes truly multifarious and illustrative. That is what I mean by liberty; give it its head and let it range. If it is in a bad way, and the English novel is, I think, nothing but absolute freedom can refresh it and restore its self-respect."

Assertions which tell us that Isabel has "an immense curiosity about life," or that, as against Osmond, she pleads "the cause of freedom," or other uses of words like "freedom," "liberty," and "knowledge" are so frequent in this novel that there is no need to collect them here. That Isabel has faith in exactly those ideals which James wants to see represented in the art of the novel is apparent from the fact that his vocabulary when talking about fiction is identical with that used to describe Isabel's ambitions and hopes. The similarity which can be inferred from this between Isabel's attitude towards experience as she sets out on her career and the novelist's attitude in his writing and observation is extremely important to any understanding of Isabel's place in *The Portrait of a Lady* and of James's place in it as her creator.

To begin with, the qualities of "absolute freedom" and comprehensiveness, which are recommended in the letter to Deerfield, are exactly what Isabel thinks she is finding when she falls in love first with Madame Merle and then with Gilbert Osmond. Part of her love for Osmond derives from her capacity to divine in him those "histories within histories," as they are called in the revision, which are a guarantee against vulgar judgments or a concern for the opinions of others. And though she has reservations about Madame Merle, she discovers in her a person who "appeared to have, in her experience, a touchstone for everything." She is sure that Madame Merle will be able to judge fairly of Henrietta, and this leads her to the admiring conclusion that

> "that is the supreme good fortune: to be in a better position
> for appreciating people than they are for appreciating you." And
> she added that this, when one considered it, was simply the
> essence of the aristocratic situation. In this light, if in none other,
> one should aim at the aristocratic situation.

The "aristocratic" is, for her, an "ideal" situation because it promises exemption from the restraints which generally hamper appreciation and because it provides the deepening experience which permits confidence and security of judgment. The advantages which Isabel has in mind are essentially those which James regarded as most desirable for a novelist. There is some likeness, as a matter of fact, between Isabel's "supreme good fortune" and James's notion of the fine central intelligence. Long before he discusses the idea in his preface, and over ten years before he wrote *The Portrait of a Lady,* he expressed the essential meaning of the concept of central intelligence in terms which, again, are like those ascribed in the novel to Isabel's ideal:

> In every human imbroglio, be it of a comic or a tragic nature,
> it is good to think of an observer standing aloof, the critic, the
> idle commentator of it all, taking notes, as we may say, in the
> interest of truth.

It is clear that Isabel is not such an observer as James here imagines, and it is precisely in the nature of her unhappiness and her betrayal that she never achieves the "situation" she admires. The similarity between James, the novelist in the novel, with his enviable position for observation, and Isabel, the heroine who tries to achieve it, explains why James is so lovingly sympathetic about her girlish eagerness at the beginning and about her failure at the end. With so congenial a subject, and one with such relevance to his intellectual autobiography, it is the more remarkable that he is able to maintain, though not with perfect consistency, the poise of the "observer standing aloof."

The style through which James expresses his role as the observer and narrator in *The Portrait of a Lady* is an indication of his security, of the achieved aristocracy of his position. This is particularly apparent in the quality of the comedy, where there is represented that ideally civilized view of experience which Isabel desires and which she fails to detect in Ralph. James's style has the characteristics, put into language, which identify Ralph as the most admirably intelligent character in the novel. He has, we are told, an inclination to "jocosity and irony," a phrase which James significantly changes in the revision to "adventure and irony." The latter words aptly describe the nature of the comedy in this novel—it is used to champion the cause of speculativeness and imagination and to expose the various seductions to which it may fall prey. James's tone, and, by his leave, Ralph's, is affectionate and encouraging, but it is also superior; it is tolerant, but it is above all self-confident. By the moderation of voice in the narrated style, particularly in the first half when Isabel is being introduced, James constrains us to habits of response and understanding that make us sympathetic observers of Isabel's career and partisans of the values to which she subscribes.

While James's voice at the opening is not identical with Ralph's, it expresses an equally amused and undefensive urbanity of mind. For a good half of the passage with which the novel begins, the tone has a quality which is characteristic of certain observable features of English conversation. There is a noticeable habit of verbal exaggeration, by which relatively small things assume extraordinary proportions, accompanied by extremely imposing discriminations about them. The total effect is close to the mock epic. The first paragraph sounds as if James were sifting the afternoon into exquisite little pieces, giving the whole description a kind of elegant prissiness:

> Under certain circumstances there are few hours in life more agreeable than the hour dedicated to the ceremony known as afternoon tea. There are circumstances in which, whether you partake of the tea or not—some people of course never do—the situation is in itself delightful. These that I have in mind in

beginning to unfold this simple history offered an admirable setting to an innocent pastime. The implements of the little feast had been disposed upon the lawn of an old English country-house, in what I should call the perfect middle of a splendid summer afternoon. Part of the afternoon had waned, but much of it was left, and what was left was of the finest and rarest quality. Real dusk would not arrive for many hours; but the flood of summer light had begun to ebb, the air had grown mellow, the shadows were long upon the smooth, dense turf. They lengthened slowly, however, and the scene expressed that sense of leisure still to come which is perhaps the chief source of one's enjoyment of such a scene at such an hour. From five o'clock to eight is on certain occasions a little eternity; but on such an occasion as this the interval could be only an eternity of pleasure.

The diction, none of which was altered in the revision, has a fastidious pomposity—"ceremony known as afternoon tea," "some people of course never do"—and we are to imagine this use of language not as part of an impersonal narration, but as a fairly personal address—note the use of "I"—from someone striking a very individual social posture. The fastidiousness and the pomposity are harmlessly and, therefore, the more amusingly expended upon an event which is by no means less delightful than he claims. But his eager discriminations, the minute measurement of the remnants of the afternoon, the repetitions of words like "such" and "certain," give an excessive and correspondingly satiric note to the ritualized feelings that are at the same time being commended. James assumes a definable role in this passage. He sounds like an overly impressed American who has "gone" English, who is more English than the English. Nonetheless, the voice teases itself, as of a man who does take delight in English habits, but with such amused and self-assured adaptability that he can exaggerate and gently spoof them.

To be aware of the stylistic accomplishment here, we need only recall for a moment certain passages in *The American*. The comparison is a natural one, not only because both novels involve the experiences in Europe of relatively untutored Americans, but also because both novels are concerned here and there with exploiting the comedy inherent in the confrontation of two cultures. In her first conversation with Newman, Madame de Bellegarde expresses her sense of opposition in a way which makes her own culture both civilized and humorously inquisitive, and transforms Newman's into one which is peculiar to the point of anthropological curiosity ("I have seen several Americans"). Her wit reveals a high cultivation and a considerable intelligence, but we are left to think that both of these are at the service of provincial assumptions about Paris and America. It takes considerable daring and confidence on James's part to allow such licence to the expression of an attractively entertaining and satiric view of the hero and his background. It is part of the weakness of *The American,* however, that ultimately James is not daring enough in his characterization of Newman, that he idealizes him, sometimes ridiculously, and that his own satiric wit is used on occasion obtrusively in Newman's favour. There is a crudity of tone, as at the engagement party, whenever James feels the need to come to his hero's defence. As a result, a comic contrast between Newman's values and those of the French, which is often given an effectively complex dramatic rendering, it turned into satiric diatribe in behalf of the hero.

The passage . . . in which James describes Newman at the Bellegardes' party has a stridency of invective which is as far from the aloofness of James's ideal commentator, or from Isabel's aristocratically perceptive observer, as the early novels ever get. The revisions in no way moderate the tone, even though they were made long after the writing of *The Portrait of a Lady.* The conclusion is obvious: at no time could the character of Newman or his perplexities engage the kind of refined and cultivated attention which James gives to Isabel Archer. Her social relationships involve for him attitudes and awarenesses that are deeply entangled in his feelings about his own relationship to the fictional world he creates. In *The American,* Newman's difficulties in French society signify little more than aspects of the European-American contrast about which his feelings were substantially simpler. They do not, as do the personal difficulties of Isabel, serve as the condition for dramatizing the psychological and moral, one is tempted to repeat the epistemological, problems which attend relationships among people who, except for Henrietta, have consciously escaped from any confinement within the European-American definition. Nowhere in the early novels, except intermittently in *The Europeans,* is James as aloof as he is here from prejudices about American and European manners. And in *The Portrait* more than in any of his other works, he reveals a capacity to be comically invigorating by playing upon and then disappointing our expectations about cultural differences.

If James's style creates an atmosphere in which there is a liberal opportunity for the most unprovincial kinds of feeling and attitude, the style of social discourse among the characters in the opening scene does no less. Indeed, if there is any question of James's highly sophisticated comic intention in his opening description, it is soon dispelled by the dramatic action which immediately follows. Far from being conscious of an "eternity of pleasure," two of the people actually taking part in the "ceremony known as afternoon tea," Ralph and Lord Warburton, are instead aware of its agreeable tedium. More than that, the host and the owner of what James calls "the peculiarly English picture" is a "shrewd American banker" drinking out of an unusually large cup, while he listens to the desultory talk of his son and his neighbour. The talk among the gentlemen establishes a condition for social discourse which blends easily into the witty virtuosity of James's introduction:

> "Warburton's tone is worse than mine [Ralph said]; he pretends to be bored; I am not in the least bored; I find life only too interesting."
> "Ah, *too* interesting [his father remarked]; you shouldn't allow it to be that, you know!"
> "I am never bored when I come here," said Lord Warburton. "One gets such uncommonly good talk."
> "Is that another sort of joke?" asked the old man. "You have no excuse for being bored anywhere. When I was your age, I had never heard of such a thing."
> "You must have developed very late."

The boredom of the young men is not a very serious matter. Like everything else in the scene it is treated as a joke, so that Mr. Touchett, not without amusement himself, complains that "you young men have too many jokes." They joke about Ralph's health, his ugliness, and Mr. Touchett's illness, about Warburton's politics, and, when old Touchett remarks that conditions are "getting more serious" in the world, about seriousness itself: "The increasing seriousness of things," Ralph remarks, "that is the great opportunity of jokes." All of the jokes reveal a high degree of self-assurance on the part of the characters, as in Warburton's remark on Mr. Touchett's "development," and, even more, a considerable confidence within the group in the intelligence and essential good-will of one another.

It can be said, then, that the social relationship among the characters at tea is not unlike the presumed relationship between James and his reader: we are all men of the world without being in the least tired of the fun offered by talking even about our boredom. The importance of the resemblance between James's tone and that of the gentlemen at tea is not merely that they are both comic in about the same ways. More significant, is that just when the social environment of the novel, the "color of its air," to use

James's phrase, comes into being as a discriminating and sophisticated one, Isabel Archer, with all her impetuosity and youthfully theoretical eagerness, is brought into the scene.

The dramatic situation can be most naturally described in a question: how are people of this sort, James the narrator as well as those at tea, who talk as they do and who have a sense of the hovering ridiculousness even of Ralph's fatal illness, how are they to respond to the entrance of a bright-eyed American girl who can carry on conversations which are often embarrassingly pretentious? With its manifestation of social and intellectual standards that are a measure for evaluating things through most of the action, the extremely moderated comic tone of the opening is also the instrument, for a good half of the novel, by which James characterizes Isabel and through which Ralph expresses his love for her. It is vitally important to see this if we are to recognize that some of Isabel's seductively phrased self-analysis is not to be taken at face value, and if we are to understand why James's characterization of her is often intentionally elusive. The chivalrousness and intelligence in his treatment of Isabel is apparent in the genially critical comedy of the voice at the opening and throughout the novel up to the point of her marriage. This is the sort of comedy which James admired in the "expressive and sympathetic smile" of Alphonse Daudet, "the smile," he wrote in 1883, "of the artist, the sceptic, the man of the world." By means of such comedy, both James and Ralph can express an amused and mature tolerance of the heroine's vagaries. And in James's style, the reader can actually *feel* that "respect for the liberty of the subject," in this case of Isabel, which he calls in "The Lesson of Balzac"—"*the* great sign of the painter of the first order."

There are two ways in which Isabel is endowed with the "freedom" which James respected so unreservedly. The first is by the practical generosity of James, as her creator, and of the Touchetts, as her benefactors; the second, by the generosity of spirit which breathes through James's style and through the social life of Gardencourt. It is characteristic of James to absolve his favourites from ordinary limitations. They are usually rich, more than normally intelligent, morally superior, and socially appealing. Isabel is all these things, except that at first she lacks the wealth and the kind of companionship by which her virtues can be adequately stimulated. By the various provisions which the Touchetts make for Isabel, James secures all the necessary practical conditions for her "freedom." This is particularly true of the fortune which Ralph arranges for the specific reason, as he tells his father, that "she wishes to be free, and your bequest will make her free." But more importantly, the Touchetts, like James himself, allow Isabel the full bent of her self-dramatizing tendencies. Each of them has a self-confident tolerance which assures Isabel that she can express herself without fear of being called to a restricting account of motive or consistency. Even Mrs. Touchett, with her somewhat unimaginative, conventional re-action to Isabel's rejection of Warburton, admits to being charmed by Isabel's independence. When Ralph is curious about what his mother plans to "do" with her, she replies that Isabel is not, after all, "a yard of calico. I shall do absolutely nothing with her, and she herself will do everything that she chooses." In this remark, as in the general conversational tone among the Touchetts, there is a characteristic toughness of mind, which, curiously enough, reveals itself in the nature of their kindness. Their gen-erosity is invariably indirect, not only when Ralph manages to give Isabel a fortune through the will of his father, but also when Mrs. Touchett lets her feel that she is paying her own expenses on the trip to Europe. Not only the fact but also the manner of their generosity is meant to free Isabel from restrictive obligation. The witty toughness of their talk with one another exempts everyone from the intimidations, the limitations of re-sponse that can result from assertions of praise or kindness that are too direct. Isabel's friendship with Mrs. Touchett begins when she greets her with "you must be our crazy Aunt Lydia," and Mr. Touchett's conver-sations with Ralph involve considerable humour, some of it rather rough, about his son's illness: "Oh no, he's not clumsy," he assures Lord War-burton in the presence of Ralph, "considering that he's an invalid himself. He's a very good nurse—for a sick nurse. I call him my sick nurse because he's sick himself." Secret generosity, the disguise of love by joking—these are the ways of Ralph, his father, and, to an extent, his mother, for letting others escape the embarrassments of obligation.

The liberation of personality which is encouraged by the social at-mosphere of Gardencourt is implicit in the comedy which permeates the dialogue. In this way the ideal of "freedom" is given dramatic and stylistic existence. We can, to repeat, actually hear and feel what it is like. This is especially true in those scenes in which Ralph and Isabel deal with the phenomenon of Henrietta Stackpole, a woman who is not only "serious" but undeviatingly fixed in her opinions. A fair sample of the kind of dis-course which Isabel thought sufficiently intelligent before she came to Gar-dencourt is offered by any one of Henrietta's remarks after she arrives there herself. Within the atmosphere of Gardencourt she becomes a comic figure even for Isabel. The urbane amplitude of mind which she encounters in Ralph drives her to ever stronger assertions of a parochial Americanism. Given the high values attached in the novel to urbanity of judgment, Henrietta is an eccentric, almost, were it not for her redeeming perceptiveness, one of James's comic grotesques. As James himself puts it in the revision, she is "the all-judging one." "Persons, in her view," Ralph thinks at one point, "were simple and homogeneous organisms." It is natural that such a person should become the comic foil to Ralph, whose attitude is summed up in his advice to Isabel: "Judge people as critics, and you will condemn them all." Much of the broadest comedy in the first half of the novel derives from the conversations between Ralph and Henrietta and the contrast between his supple and extemporizing mind and her attempts to confine him within the limits of her doctrinaire and superficial categories:

> "I don't suppose that you are going to undertake to persuade me that *you* are an American," she said.
> "To please you, I will be an Englishman, I will be a Turk!"
> "Well, if you can change about that way, you are very welcome," Miss Stackpole rejoined.

Her misconceptions of Ralph include an inability to understand the mildly ironic joking that plays through all his conversation, and at one point she even accuses him to Isabel of having insulted her with the imputation that she had proposed to him. It is indicative of James's talent for inventing comic parallels to the more portentous elements in his stories that Isabel should tell Ralph about this misunderstanding. She thereby becomes involved in a joking attitude towards the subject of marriage proposals and of European attitudes towards women just two chapters before her rejection of Warburton, when these same matters will provoke her to confused and painful self-scrutiny:

> Ralph stared. "Has she complained of me?"
> "She told me she thinks there is something very low in the tone of Europeans towards women."
> "Does she call me a European?"
> "One of the worst. She told me you said to her something that an American never would have said. But she didn't repeat it."
> Ralph treated himself to a burst of resounding laughter.

Isabel's capacity to take a large view of Henrietta's eccentricity, to acknowledge her silliness and yet remain affectionately loyal to her, is due not simply to the sharper awareness of social and intellectual qualities which comes from her contacts with Ralph and his friends. Rather, it results from the *manner* in which Ralph prods her into this awareness. The scene in which this is most charmingly dramatized indicates two very important things about the quality of literary expression in the novel whenever Isabel is being shown in a critical light. The first of these is the way James permits Ralph to exercise a comic playfulness, a capacity to avoid all obvious pedagogical seriousness, thereby allowing Isabel to come painlessly and with only pleasurable embarrassment to a recognition of her own absurdities. The second is James's ability to "take care" of his heroine without resorting to the blatancies and idealizations which have been noted in *The American*. The tone allows for that "adventure and irony" in response to Isabel which is both for Ralph and James the guarantee of a sceptical idealism. When she discusses Henrietta with Ralph her sentimental view of her friend's nationality is expressed in language reminiscent of Henrietta's own verbal habits:

> "Well," said Isabel, smiling, "I am afraid it is because she is rather vulgar that I like her."
>
> "She would be flattered by your reason!"
>
> "If I should tell her, I would not express it in that way. I should say it is because there is something of the 'people' in her."
>
> "What do you know about the people? and what does she, for that matter?"
>
> "She knows a great deal, and I know enough to feel that she is a kind of emanation of the great democracy—of the continent, the country, the nation. I don't say that she sums it up, that would be too much to ask of her. But she suggests it; she reminds me of it."
>
> "You like her then for patriotic reasons. I am afraid it is on those very grounds that I object to her."
>
> "Ah," said Isabel, with a kind of joyous sigh, "I like so many things! If a thing strikes me in a certain way, I like it. I don't want to boast, but I suppose I am rather versatile. I like people to be totally different from Henrietta—in the style of Lord Warburton's sisters, for instance. So long as I look at the Misses Molyneux, they seem to me to answer a kind of ideal. Then Henrietta presents herself, and I am immensely struck with her; not so much for herself as what stands behind her.
>
> "Ah, you mean the back view of her," Ralph suggested.
>
> "What she says is true," his cousin answered; "you will never be serious. I like the great country stretching away beyond the rivers and across the prairies, blooming and smiling and spread-

ing, till it stops at the blue Pacific! A strong, sweet, fresh odour seems to rise from it, and Henrietta—excuse my simile—has something of that odour in her garments."

Isabel blushed a little as she concluded this speech, and the blush, together with the momentary ardour she had thrown into it, was so becoming to her that Ralph stood smiling at her for a moment after she had ceased speaking.

"I am not sure the Pacific is blue," he said; "but you are a woman of imagination. Henrietta, however, is fragrant—Henrietta is decidedly fragrant."

The civilized sweetness of Ralph's temperament and the loving gentleness of his pleasure in her artless enthusiasm is never more ingratiatingly dramatized than here, and the passage ought to be kept in mind when, in Rome, we see Isabel as the wife and hostess of Gilbert Osmond: "She was dressed in black velvet; she looked brilliant and noble." There, she is representing her husband; here she is expressing herself. In this exchange, she learns to see the absurdity of her speech without anyone needing to remark it. In the revision, however, James makes a point of having her description of Henrietta and America carry even more of a comic burden. For the statement that Henrietta "reminds" her of the continent, James substitutes the line "she vividly figures it"; for Isabel's statement that she likes what "stands behind" Henrietta, he later provides the phrase "masses behind." Both changes allow Ralph's remark about "the back view of her" to become exorbitantly funny. The possibility of a human being representing something or someone else, which bears, as I suggest, on what happens eventually to Isabel, and which will be discussed [elsewhere] at some length, is here the object of comic ridicule. Henrietta becomes in Isabel's description a grotesquely literal representation of the size and smell of the whole American continent.

Needless to say, the comedy is to serious purpose. This calls quite explicitly for definition, however, when Isabel repeats to Ralph the erroneous charge so often made by Henrietta: "You will never be serious." The ultimate sadness of her situation is that while she sees in Ralph a capacity for appreciation not unlike that which makes her fall in love with Osmond, she cannot recognize in the humour with which he expresses it the guarantee that, with him, her own tastes and predelictions will not be insidiously stifled. She chooses Osmond, and after three years of marriage comes to the discovery that "he took himself so seriously; it was something appalling." Her failure is in her incapacity to see the significance of comedy.

No wonder that she mistakes in Osmond the virtues that belong to Ralph. The similarity created between the two men is another instance of James's capacity to evoke the complexity of moral choice by showing the correspondences between the admirable and the corrupt. A measure of his genius is his ability to prove dramatically that no personal characteristic is of itself necessarily good or evil except within the structure of a particular personality. Osmond is made into Ralph Touchett *in extremis,* and Isabel may remark that

> Ralph had something of this same quality, this appearance of thinking that life was a matter of connoisseurship; but in Ralph it was an anomaly, a kind of humorous excrescence, whereas in Mr. Osmond it was the key-note, and everything was in harmony with it.

"Everything was in harmony with it"—in that phrase, carrying implications of a systematic measuring and "placing" of experience, is the secret of the essential difference between Ralph's connoisseurship and Osmond's. Ralph may be a connoisseur, but his expression of this has a comicality which suggests the reverse of a desire to make everything harmonious with the prejudices of his own taste. As against Osmond's insistent reduction of Isabel's individuality to the service of his egoism, there is the always liberating humour of Ralph. He allows her the fullest liberty of expression, imposing nothing upon her but the smiles and the wit of which her own blushes, even before he speaks, admit the necessity and the justice.

II

The ambience which is provided for Isabel at the beginning of the novel is a perfect achievement of James's theories about the sort of existence which a novelist ought to allow his heroines. As her creator, he gives Isabel a kind of freedom which Balzac provides for Madame Marneffe and Thackeray denies his Becky Sharp. James himself best explains the significance of this in "The Lesson of Balzac." The passage shows once more his dedication to a terminology about character which I have put to considerable use:

> "Balzac aime sa Valérie," says Taine, in his great essay—so much the finest thing ever written on our author—speaking of the way in which the awful little Madame Marneffe of *Les Parents Pauvres* is drawn, and of the long rope, for her acting herself out, that

her creator's participation in her reality assures her. He has been contrasting her, as it happens, with Thackeray's Becky Sharp or rather with Thackeray's attitude toward Becky, and the marked jealousy of her freedom that Thackeray exhibits from the first. I remember reading at the time of the publication of Taine's study—though it was long, long ago—a phrase in an English review of the volume which seemed to my limited perception, even in extreme youth, to deserve the highest prize ever bestowed on critical stupidity undisguised. If Balzac loved his Valérie, said this commentator, that only showed Balzac's extraordinary taste; the truth being really, throughout, that it was just through this love of each seized identity, and of the sharpest and liveliest identities most, that Madame Marneffe's creator was able to marshal his array at all. The love, as we call it, the joy in their communicated and exhibited movement, in their standing on their feet and going of themselves and acting out their characters, was what rendered possible the saturation [with his ideas] I speak of; what supplied him, through the inevitable gaps of his preparation and the crevices of his prison, his long prison of labor, short cut to the knowledge he required. It was by loving them—as the terms of his subject and the nuggets of his mine—that he knew them; it was not by knowing them that he loved.

Balzac, he continues, protected his heroine "in the interest of her special genius and freedom," and he contrasts this with what he calls Thackeray's "moral eagerness," his desire, "to make sure, first of all, of your moral judgment."

The relevance of these ideas to the presentation of character in James's early novels is obvious enough. James's problem, briefly, is to avoid sacrificing the complexity or richness of character in the interest of moral edification or the representation of abstract qualities. This is a particularly crucial matter, since as a novelist James is also anxious to avoid subverting the emblematic qualities of his characters by overly strenuous psychological definition of motive. Complexity for him resides in action motivated by the most intense moral consciousness, and this often has little to do with what we now consider psychological motivation. Since James's judgments of such action are expressed largely through the comedy, the problem of the evaluation of character and its "exposure" is, very often, one of comic tone. While this is a matter of literary technique, it has its source in James's own personal morality. For that reason the problem of judgment becomes, as we have seen, not only a dramatic circumstance within the action of the novel, but also the observable condition in the style through which the action is given life. Dr. Sloper of *Washington Square* reveals what it means to use comedy not as an expression of tenderness but of an undeviating and arrogant judgment. His comedy is full of sarcasm, and it is significant that James in an early essay on Turgenev expresses the opinion that the ultimate novelist should be "purged" of just that quality. Though Turgenev could occasionally "forswear his irony and become frankly sympathetic," he could do so only in his conceptions of women, and his besetting limitation was that his ironic temper led him to the excess of seeing all human aspiration with a ruthless pessimism. James used the word "irony" at the time of the essay on Turgenev, 1874, as a synonym for "sarcasm," and it indicated what he took to be a notion in Turgenev's novels that there was something conclusively vain in human effort.

Quite another sort of irony, observable in the passages just discussed from *The Portrait of a Lady,* provides the means by which James and such humorously minded heroes as Ralph avoid being "sarcastic." The comedy in this novel, as it comes from the Touchetts in the opening chapters and from James's narration, allows Isabel unencumbered liberty of expression and theoretical aspiration. Both from sickly and ugly Ralph and from his dying father the presumption is in favour of the brighter side of things. It is clear from the exchange between Ralph and Isabel about Henrietta, for instance, that some of the comedy in the novel is meant to show the extreme youthfulness and intellectual immaturity of the heroine. Far from being sarcastic about these, however, the comedy tends to make us take pleasure in them.

Ralph, Mr. Touchett, Warburton, and Madame Merle are people of great verbal exactness, so much so that their wit depends on twisting whatever is conventionally phrased into a joke. One consequence, created by the maturely intelligent social life in the novel, is that some of Isabel's conversation sounds like that of a young girl imitating what she mistakenly believes to be intellectually sophisticated talk. This is most endearingly evident when she addresses remarks such as, "Oh, I do hope they will make a revolution! I should delight in seeing a revolution," to an auditor who is as kindly and graciously playful as Mr. Touchett. Though he tells her that he has heard her "take such opposite views," he does not hold her to any strict accountability for them. And neither does James, a fact which can explain the difficulty and the peculiarity of this novel.

James's insistence on Isabel's "freedom" from accountability even to herself for the resolution and explanation of vague, often contradictory statements extends to those parts of the novel in which he characterizes her by his own, often symbolically suggestive descriptions. To take an instance often discussed, we are told that in Albany she likes to read alone in a room which she chooses for its atmosphere of mysterious melancholy and which is secured from the outside street by a bolted door whose sidelights have been filled with green paper. "But she had no wish to look out," James continues, "for this would have interfered with her theory that there was a strange, unseen place on the other side—a place which became, to the child's imagination, according to its different moods, a region of delight or of terror." The peculiarity and inventiveness of detail encourage inferences that Isabel is displaying something more than the usual pleasures of a child in picturesque and remote parts of a house. The passage demands attention and determines the focus of many readers because it seems to provide a key, if one is looking at the scene in terms of the completed action of the novel, to the eventual difficulties of the heroine. "Isabel's history is prefigured," writes Mr. Quentin Anderson, "in the image of her speculation before the locked door of the 'office' in Albany." The locked room is an image, he claims, of Isabel's "self-absorption," and it is only Osmond's proposal, ironically enough, which "makes possible the opening of a long closed door."

The notion that Isabel is self-absorbed involves the kind of denominated judgment which the whole tone of her characterization warns us against, and quite explicitly at one point when the matter is affectionately disposed of with the remark that "you could have made her blush, any day in the year, by telling her that she was selfish," or, as the revision has it, "a rank egoist." There are few of us, however, faced with the obliquity of this novel who have not at one time or other agreed with Mr. Anderson's reading of this passage and with his ascription of its significance to the novel as a whole. In disagreeing with him, I am concerned not with what we may imagine about a character like Isabel but rather with the fact that the quality of expression in the novel informs us that we may imagine many things but that we are not to believe all of them. The image of the room in Albany does lend itself to translation into a "portrait" of Isabel which is what Mr. Anderson says it is, but it could also give a very different one. Either can be sustained by the novel as a whole. Why read the passage as indicating self-absorption or the tendency to see "delight" and "terror" as exclusive alternatives? We could as easily read it, both in view of later action and in its immediate context, as suggesting Isabel's capacity, even in a place as unstimulating as Albany, to imagine experience of a more heightened and colourful kind than her actual situation warrants. Given the kind of expression to which the novel as a whole is dedicated, we cannot translate the implications of this passage into a characterizing term that "fixes" Isabel Archer. She admits, as a matter of fact, to being "absorbed in myself." This admission is merely an experimental and moralistic self-deprecation, however, and it derives from aspects of her character which are important to James's conception of the overall meanings of the novel. He alludes to these when he tells us that "she is always planning out her own development, desiring her own perfection, observing her own progress." She has a novelist's interest in herself, though, as Mr. Richard Chase observes, it is that of a novelist more romantic than James. To say this is to describe a *process* in her thinking. This is an important task in a novel which is everywhere concerned with kinds of consciousness, and it brings us closer to its dramatic centre than do terms, like "self-absorbed," which are predicated upon the assumption that we are dealing with a character already formed rather than in the process of forming herself.

Isabel is continually making statements about herself which are, if we ignore the social atmosphere of the novel, as tempting to the reader who is seeking explanations as is the locked door in Albany. The style and plausibility of her remarks often sound, indeed, like authentic summations, such as a commentator might make upon a character. A good example, which incidentally has the same burden as the passage on Albany, is her conversation with Ralph about "experience":

> "You want to see life, as the young men say."
> "I don't think I want to see it as the young men want to see it; but I do want to look about me."
> "You want to drain the cup of experience."
> "No, I don't wish to touch the cup of experience. It's a poisoned drink! I only want to see for myself."
> "You want to see, but not to feel," said Ralph.
> "I don't think that if one is a sentient being, one can make the distinction," Isabel returned.

The peculiarity of this passage, and of many like it, is, to repeat, that the vocabulary is like a novelist's in his presentation of a character or like a literary critic's when he is discussing one. The difference is that a literary critic or a novelist, unless he were assuming a dramatic role, would not be allowed to talk as carelessly and vaguely as Isabel does. The drift of her remarks leads understandably to Ralph's assertion that she wants "to see, but not to feel," and yet she is allowed simply to pull out from under this with her reply that such a thing is impossible. One can, of course, work out what she has in mind: she can feel something about what she sees without taking a more active participation in it. But the product of our interpretation is less to the point than the quality of her language, which makes any interpretation slightly untrustworthy. It is in keeping with the intentions of the novel as a dramatic form to leave Isabel's terms as vague as they are, and to see in their elusiveness, rather than in the meanings we can derive by translating them into quite other terms, a revelation of her character. Thus, on the basis of her remarks to Ralph we could say *not* that she is a girl who wants to see life and is afraid of directly experiencing it, but that she is a girl whose attempts to explain her position result in a fuzzy use of language. We can say further that the position itself could be taken as a rationalization for a confusion of impulses, a confusion which is apparent both in her conduct in Albany and in her way of talking about herself.

It will be crucial to the final appraisal which is to be given the novel in this [essay], that the inferences about Isabel's psychological peculiarity which we can draw from such passages as those I have been discussing are not allowed in the total structure to make us at all cynical about her vocabulary of "freedom." We cannot, without changing the rhythm and direction of the novel, decide that her general love of liberty is really a fear of the realities of particular experience. James does give us, however, a very tentative suggestion about Isabel which, if developed in conjunction with all that is fully achieved, would have, for me at least, made the novel a greater work than it is. I refer to the implication that there can be no such thing as the "freedom" which Isabel wants and which Ralph and James want for her, simply for the reason that regardless of opportunity in the world outside, there are in everyone the flaws, the fears, the neuroses that fix and confine and stifle.

In admitting the defects of his heroine, and in suggesting others, James manages to put us in a state of mind in which we agree that they are mostly the function of age and inexperience. He warns us quite explicitly about the vulgarity of using "scientific criticism" on a girl who is so unformed and so promising:

> Altogether, with her meagre knowledge, her inflated ideals, her confidence at once innocent and dogmatic, her temper at once exacting and indulgent, her mixture of curiosity and fastidiousness, of vivacity and indifference, her desire to look well and to be if possible even better; her determination to see, to try, to

know; her combination of the delicate, desultory, flame-like spirit and the eager and personal young girl; she would be an easy victim of scientific criticism, if she were not to awaken on the reader's part an impulse more tender and more purely expectant.

This exhortation is full of very strong feeling. The abrupt and over-lapping changes of tone indicate James's anxious desire to convince the reader that for all the oddities he may see in Isabel, he is to love her the more and to engage the less in any attempt to sum her up. Balzac *aime sa Valérie* and James his Isabel. Part of the "freedom" we allow her is the use of her abstract and self-aggrandizing vocabulary, the very pretentiousness of which is, in part, what makes us "tender and more purely expectant."

James's contrivance in allowing Isabel to act without any specification of motive is particularly provocative because the novel is concerned throughout with the possibilities of marriage—with Isabel's acceptance or rejection of certain qualities represented in her suitors and with her reasons for doing so. Considering this, we come upon the connection between the quality of some of the social satire in the novel and the permissiveness in James's relationship to his heroine.

Briefly, he prefers to make her choice of a husband a sign of her superiority to customary social values rather than indicative of deeply psychological motive. Any possibility of directing social satire against Isabel for her rejection of an English lord is explicitly declined by James, and, indeed, very directly purged from the reader's mind. Throughout chapter 12, where he dramatizes Isabel's difficulties over Warburton's proposal, he eschews the kind of satire which derives its standards from what he calls "the more quickly-judging half of mankind." He is referring to qualities in the responses of all his readers which are conditioned by what are presumably the social "facts of life." Isabel herself gives an instance of these when she admits that Warburton's proposal represents a "magnificent 'chance,' " and throughout the chapter James goes to considerable effort to include the attitudes of the "judging" world. He does so, however, only in the process of telling us of their inadequacy and in warning the reader that if he adopts them he cannot possibly understand Isabel's problem or her decision. All he would be able to do is to view her satirically. Having told us at the beginning that Isabel anticipates the proposal, James observes that "it may appear to some readers that the young lady was both precipitate and unduly fastidious, but the latter of these facts, if the charge be true, may serve to exonerate her from the discredit of the former."

This is followed by an equally disciplinary assault on the reader who might view Isabel's problem from the generally accepted social assumption that an orphaned American girl in need of a fortune must be in want of an English lord. "At the risk of making the reader smile, is must be said that there had been moments when the intimation that she was admired by a "personage" struck her as an aggression which she would rather have been spared." Not content with issuing these warnings nor with the fact that in the scene on the lake between Ralph and Henrietta he has already indicated a capacity, when he thinks it appropriate, to dramatize the comic and satiric possibilities of a young lady's presumptions about European proposals of marriage, James is so concerned that we may treat his heroine's uncertainty from the narrow view of social advantage that he resorts to what he himself regarded as a Trollopean misdemeanour. He violates the historical tone of the novel and "winks at us and reminds us that he is telling us an arbitrary thing":

> Smile not, however, I venture to repeat, at this simple young woman from Albany, who debated whether she should accept an English peer before he had offered himself, and who was disposed to believe that on the whole she could do better. She was a person of great good faith, and if there was a great deal of folly in her wisdom, those who judge her severely may have the satisfaction of finding that, later, she became consistently wise only at the cost of an amount of folly which will constitute almost a direct appeal to charity.

It is plain enough from James's remark on Trollope, and from the regard he expresses in the prefaces for the benefits of suspense in a wholly dramatic rendering of experience, that James writes as he does in this passage because he is writing under a compulsion. He writes in a manner not most pleasing to his art, an example of which is illustrated in the style, with its implications of comic detachment, that we find in the opening chapter. Here, in chapter 12, it is as if our view of his heroine was seriously threatened by the intrusions of standards totally unlike those created in the first paragraph of the novel, as if the impositions of a "vulgar world" might overwhelm the author's customarily ironic and urbane voice. He is not ironic himself, and he warns us against being so, against the "smile." The significance of this is obvious once it is recognized that the "smile" is only a symptom of something to which he is even more opposed: the judgments of what are referred to throughout the chapter as the "public at large," the "multitude," the "more quickly judging half of mankind," as these things are possibly exemplified in us. James is trying to protect Isabel from a certain kind of irony simply by telling us that if we choose to smile at her it is because we fail to see that her response to Warburton's proposal is more complicated than are our customary social preconceptions about the opportunity she is offered. Lord Warburton himself is aware that his proposal to a girl who has neither beauty nor wealth and whom he has seen for no more than twenty odd hours is not the kind of action that "justifies a man to the multitude." Being who he is, however, he can quite easily dismiss such thoughts from his mind. It is not so easy for Isabel, and her difficulties in disentangling her feelings from what other people might think of them attests to how far she is, at this point, from the ideal of the "aristocratic situation." Her perplexity leads her even to the making of statements which she does not mean, so that at one point she tells Warburton that she cannot believe that his proposal is serious:

> These words of Isabel's were not perfectly sincere, for she had no doubt whatever that he was serious. They were simply a tribute to the fact, of which she was perfectly aware, that those he himself had just uttered would have excited surprise on the part of the public at large.

James's admiration for Isabel expends itself most enthusiastically upon her attempts to get away from the need to "pay tribute" to the public at large. It is because she finds herself paying such a tribute, even in discussing, much less deciding upon Warburton's proposal, that she rejects him. Mr. F. R. Leavis remarks that her refusal "doesn't strike us as the least capricious," and he stresses the importance of the "lapse" in taste when Warburton, in chapter 7, asks Mrs. Touchett is Isabel might stay up alone with the gentlemen. According to Mr. Leavis, Warburton's conduct "brings to a concrete point for us the rightness of her decision against him." But since the "lapse," if it is one, is brought to our attention by Mrs. Touchett, it is at least arguable that we are not to place as much emphasis on it as Mr. Leavis does, particularly when we consider that Mrs. Touchett's objections to Isabel's visit to London bring forth comment from James that:

> Like many ladies of her country who have lived a long time in Europe, she had completely lost her native tact on such points, and in her reaction, not in itself deplorable, against the liberty allowed to young persons beyond the seas, had fallen into gratuitous and exaggerated scruples.

I am not primarily interested in correcting Mr. Leavis's reading of this particular passage, which has been widely accepted. Rather, my purpose here, as in the discussion of Mr. Quentin Anderson's interpretation of the scene in Albany, is to show in a particular instance that an explanation of Isabel's conduct or of a character like Warburton cannot safely be made in terms that are as objective and specific as those which usually satisfy James's critics. Upon this matter depends one's entire understanding of Isabel's conduct and of what James is saying in his presentation of her. She herself is confused about her reasons for doing things, because at this stage in the novel she is intimidated, despite her talk about "freedom," by constricting social customs which seem to make her reticence publicly absurd. As a result, the chapter represents her attempts to find now one and now another explanation for her intuition that she cannot marry him. All her reasons add up to one thing: she cannot marry him because by every consideration which has meaning in the social world from which she comes and in the society which, by marriage to Warburton, she would enter, it appears absolutely logical that she should.

Warburton offers her something that neither Caspar, nor Osmond, nor Ralph could offer; he is the one man in her life who belongs to a discernably organized society. It is just that which she rejects in declining his offer of marriage—conventionalized society and all that it implies about "system" in human effort and conduct. This seems to be what is meant by having her allude to his "system" in close conjunction with a reference to him as a "social magnate." It is therefore relevant to her choice that he is the only person in the novel, except for the innocuous Bantling, who is not an expatriate, and that he is also the only person who, manifesting a belief in public action, is seriously political. That he is interested in politics at all, rather than the nature of his political liberalism, is what explains the otherwise peculiar emphasis on politics in Isabel's mind when she considers his proposal. To put it perhaps too emphatically, it might be said that Isabel's rejection of him is a repudiation of constituted society in the interests of an idealism of the self and of its sufficiency. In so far as it can be defined by her aspirations and her actions, "freedom" for Isabel means that she need feel responsible only to the good opinion she can have of herself and not to the judgments of anyone else.

The significance of Isabel's detachment from social "system," in the sense of her independence from its prejudices and suppositions, bears heavily upon the brilliant achievement in this novel as it involves James's autobiographical sympathy with her. The road to her ruin is paved with James's good intentions as well as her own. "Her general disposition," expressed in her interview with Warburton, is "to elude any obligation to take a restricted view." In like manner, James's "disposition" in the dramatization of her career is to be completely above any of the restrictions imposed by conventional social prejudice or national provinciality. This expresses itself at the beginning of the novel in the charming civility of tone which is intended to breed us, as it were, to the point where we will regard other experiences in the novel with attitudes equally civilized. Along with this, the comic rendering of the crudities of henrietta on the subjects of England, America, and marriage have the effect of suppressing any response to Isabel's actions which depend upon a suspicion that she is equally crude. We are to regard her choices as evolving from an almost Platonic idealism about human possibility. At the point in the novel where this idealism is offered what seems like a fairly satisfactory social realization, James becomes uncertain of the dependability of his reader. The delicate poise of his comedy is forsworn, and he appeals directly to us not to "smile" at Isabel. The reason for his anxiety lest we find her conduct eccentrically amusing is clear enough: Isabel is expressing in her *actions,* as well as by her vocabulary, those very values of independence from social confinement which provide the basis for James's own ironic superiority of tone in his style.

Organizing an Ado

Laurence Bedwell Holland

> *So I seem to have arrived at this: doubtless I have methods, but they begot themselves, in which case I am their proprietor, not their father.*
> MARK TWAIN, *The Art of Authorship*

> *Keep thy Shop, and thy Shop will keep thee.*
> BEN FRANKLIN, *Poor Richard Improved*

I

The Portraits Preface

The word "ado," even when expanded to the more impressive phrase "ado about something," is a strangely frivolous term for what James named on other occasions the "Action" of a novel, or for what, over a stretch of nine pages in the preface to *The Portrait of a Lady,* he refused to call by the name he thought "nefarious," its " 'plot.' " Indeed frivolity may be (on my part) too mild a word when we recall that the *Portrait*'s ado entails, among other things, the arrangement of a large endowment of money, a fraudulent deception, and a disastrous marriage for its heroine. Yet frivolity is often enough the acknowledged index of anxious concern rather than the mask or denial of it, and one need not assume that James was hiding something (from himself or his readers) nor imagine that he was evading an important issue when he wrote carefully of "organizing an ado about Isabel Archer." The preface sets that remark in the virtual center of a highly metaphorical context; the essay is important not primarily as an explicit argument nor

From *The Expense of Vision: Essays on the Craft of Henry James.* © 1964 by Princeton University Press.

39

even as a statement of intentions but as a sensitive exploration, employing the instrument of metaphor, which moves beneath the more explicit discourse of the preface, refining and at times running counter to it. Its full relevance to the *Portrait,* and its brilliance as an essay in its own right, come to light only when read with full attention to its metaphorical details and to the intimate drama which moves implicitly within the more explicit argument. It becomes a conscience-stricken inquiry into the deepest implications of James's craft, undertaken at a time when, in preparing the revisions for the New York edition of his fiction, James had engaged his mature creative powers in a direct confrontation of his imaginative work. What the preface can help us to see, if we follow the admittedly "long way round" it takes to get to its turning point, is that this process, a form of self-recognition for the artist, is central to the novel itself.

Indeed, the process of self-recognition is more penetrating in the *Portrait* than in the critical essays, or even those stories which deal with professional artists as particular cases, where we might be more tempted to look for it. And the *Portrait* speaks with the firm authority of a masterpiece and accordingly affords a commanding perspective on those occasions in James's career when he penetrated most deeply into his resources, his material and talent. It enables us to reexamine the connections among James's moral, social, and aesthetic themes in the light of his concern for form and to redefine James's relation to the society which has had to be interested, whether eagerly or reluctantly, in making and remaking things, in measuring the cost of human institutions and aspirations.

Of the many images of the artist which James employed, one of his favorites and most famous is that of the architect, but James's treatment of it in the preface to the *Portrait* accords it a curiously dubious status: the image does reveal some of James's deepest apprehensions about the act of imaginative vision but remains silent on the issue of "action" or the "nefarious" plot which most troubled him. The writer as architect, in his more public and active role, builds his structure, piling "brick upon brick" until, "scrupulously fitted together and packed in," they form the "large building" of the *Portrait.* The famous passage about the "house of fiction" develops the architectural image more amply, assigning to the artist a more private position inside a completed building and the ostensibly more restful occupation of a "watcher" whose sole activity is to observe: the "consciousness of the artist" stands behind the "dead wall" of a building enclosing him, equipped "with a pair of eyes, or at least with a field-glass," and scrutinizes life through the window of his particular literary form.

These architectural metaphors are relevant to the *Portrait*—if for no other reason than that they place the author *inside* his finished dwelling and call into question his edifice by alluding to its "dead wall"—yet the image of architecture does not dominate the preface because it does not satisfactorily come to grips with the assertion which James made the basis for the explicit argument of the preface. This is the assertion that the "figure" of Isabel (whatever its origin in James's acquaintanceship or reading) came first and alone without involvement in setting or action, an "unattached character" who was "not engaged in the tangle, to which we look for much of the impress that constitutes an identity." She was a "single character" given alone, as Turgenev had claimed his own were given, without the "situations" and "complications" which launch novels into "movement" and which identify a hero's world or "fate." The problem for the writer was, later, to "imagine, to invent and select and piece together" the figure's world and "destiny."

James had described this strategy before, as being Turgenev's, in his essay of 1884 on the Russian. It was based on the priority of character over "plot" and consisted in deriving the action "from the qualities of the actors" rather than from a "preconceived" plan. Its antithesis, as James then formulated it, was the novel with the *imposed* form of a *story* or "dance—a series of steps . . . determined from without and forming a figure," a strategy whose very weakness was the basis of its appeal: that of reminding readers "enough, without reminding them too much, of life." The "architecture" was *associated* loosely with plotted action as the great asset that both Scott and Balzac, unlike Turgenev, could add to their "precious material." In the late preface to the *Portrait,* however, the metaphor of architecture is *opposed,* in James's analysis, to the *action* of the novel or story. Moreover, it fails to govern the argument which James makes explicit.

The architectural images do not, for one thing, precisely locate or place Isabel. (Was she part of the structure, or did she stand, "in perfect isolation," as a center around which the "spacious house" was constructed, or was she the "plot of ground" on which the edifice was built?) Neither could architecture account for the "ado" about Isabel and the need to excite the reader's interest by the acts of characters who surround her: when thinking of the novel's action and characters in relation to "the reader's amusement," James swiftly abandoned buildings and summoned up "Roman candles and Catherine-wheels."

The language of fireworks, however, was but a momentary seizure. James immediately set aside the question of the reader's excitement and confined himself to the questions of action and character without reference to the reader; and in writing that he simply awoke one day "in possession" of the characters who were "the concrete terms of my 'plot' " he had returned to the terms of discourse, basically metaphorical in function, which actually carry the burden of the essay's searching inquiry. The terms prove in James's handling to be adequate to the resources of inspiration and method which literature shares with other arts while being more distinctly literary than architecture and fireworks; and some carry psychological implications while being tangibly institutional. Without suppressing or obscuring their multiplicity of reference, the preface underscores certain particular metaphorical connotations: they are either literary ("actors," "characters," "figure," "fable") or commercial ("peddlar," "contract," " 'tip' "). In the case of "possession," *disponible,* "agents," and "business," they prove to be both.

In attempting to trace the "growth in one's imagination" of the germ of his novel (to reconstruct "the history of the business," as James put it alternatively), James left the reader standing before a dead wall which was, in part at least, part of James's own construction. He did not name the prototype in actual life of any of his characters. In the case of the Touchetts, their friend Madame Merle, her lover Gilbert Osmond and their daughter Pansy—those who helped to awaken the novel's heroine and to arrange her marriage—James had declared that his memory was "a blank as to how and whence they came," that he simply "waked up one morning in possession of them." On the other hand, the "grasp of a single character" that inspired the novel was an act whose origin James recalled but chose not to retrace. The figure of Isabel was simply "an acquisition," tormenting in its fascination of long standing, by now rendered "familiar" but not at all "blurred" in its "charm" for having been in James's "complete possession" for "a long time."

For all the characters, then, what the preface does is not to identify their actual prototypes but, by returning repeatedly to the question of their origin, to define James's relation to them as materials, chosen or given, for his novel. The preface becomes simultaneously technical and intimately personal, as concerned with the relation of Henry James to his "setting" as with Isabel's to hers, and troubled by the phenomenon which is the essay's subject: namely the process by which resources, thematic and moral, and the pressures of actual life, from within and without, become the developing design of art. It is to this problem that the preface returns again and again in its tacking movement, every shift of which is significant, from the notations of publishing data and the recollections of Venice, which open the essay, to the last paragraphs with their acknowledged admiration for two of the novel's scenes and their apology for having overdone one character in an effort to be entertaining. The more deeply the essay probes this problem, the more troubled it is, and the more it depends on one of James's most congenial vocabularies, the language of commerce.

The imagery of trade was of some use in assessing the merits of the finished novel, for while James could admire its spaciousness as architecture, he could also praise its "economy" and compare the excitement of Isabel's meditation scene to certain staples of adventure fiction, the capture of a "caravan or the identification of a pirate." But the imagery of commerce is used chiefly to provide a setting for the artist himself, placing him in relation to his society and in relation to the "ado" about Isabel. This is the task which the opening paragraphs assume by dwelling, with little ostensible pretext, on the enticements of Venice, where James had passed a mere "several weeks," as he remembered it, of the more than a year and a half he had spent writing the *Portrait*. In the attractions of the Venetian scene he had sought inspiration for the right phrase and "next happy twist of my subject," but he had had to acknowledge that the scenes of Italy were "too rich in their own right" to perform that service; it was "as if he were asking an army of glorious veterans to help him arrest a pedlar who has given him the wrong change." Better, on reconsideration, to work in more "neutral" surroundings to which "we writers may lend something of the light of our vision." But Venice is too proud for the "charity," as James called it, of a loan. She prefers to initiate transactions: to give outright munificent gifts, for instance. But to "profit" by them the writer must either be idly "off duty" or bound to Venice's exclusive service. The novel at hand had nothing to do with Venice's service (its settings lie elsewhere), but there were, nevertheless, rewards; the transactions simply proved to be more compli- cated. To turn to Venice is "wasted effort," but nonetheless "strangely fertilizing"; "cheated and squandered" the effort always is, whether by "high-handed insolent frauds" or by "insidious sneaking ones." The issue depends on *"how"* the attention has been beguiled, but the preface does not stipulate a preferred way; suffice it that even on the most astute "designing artist's part," try as he does to "guard him against their deceits," there is "always witless enough good faith" and "anxious enough desire" to render him the dupe of such deceptions.

The process of writing is placed by this reminiscence in a context where the author may be shortchanged by his work but will not ask help from a world engrossed in larger preoccupations; where a loan, even if a "charity," is humiliating; where the free gifts of life are the rewards only of idle indulgence or of a constricted service; where the writer's precautions against fraud are merged ambivalently with a desire to be cheated; and where gains for art may possibly accrue through being wasted and defrauded.

It is against that setting of profit, swindling, and wastage that James proceeded in precisely the next sentence to deny that his novel originated in "the conceit of a 'plot,' nefarious name," though eight pages later, by using the term, he conceded that the *Portrait* does have one. But now he declared that the *given* was not an action that "launches a novel immediately into movement" but the isolated figure of Isabel. James's scruples clearly go beyond disapproval of melodramatic contrivances or the flimsy intrigues of poorly made well-made plays and call into question the very function of *plot*. Moreover, they render the discussion of the relation of character to action more urgent than was the case in the earlier essay on Turgenev because they call into question the ground of James's responsibility for his *own* novel. Impelled by this concern, the preface proceeds through the paragraphs that discuss the relation between morals and art. It avoids settling for either of two complex alternatives but is haunted and quickened by both. First: that authorship consists in the initiation of an action; that an author's responsibility stems from the creation of that action; and that to organize the *Portrait's* particular plot around Isabel Archer is in itself reprehensible. The second alternative: that authorship consists not in beginning anything but in the careful arrangement of given materials; and that to "place" and draw out the given subject of a portrait leaves the author detached and morally unaccountable for its consequences. The preface analyzes and refines the question as it approaches the point later where it can speak of the "ado about Isabel," its anxiety acknowledged and mastered because it has already discovered, in the figure of a shopkeeper, the image which gives both the terms "ado" and "plot" their precise connotations.

The essay proceeds from Venice to establish the central figure's given isolation and, with Turgenev's help, to insist that the imagination selects not simply any situations and complications for its heroes but those most "favorable to the sense of the creatures themselves, the complications they would be most likely to produce and feel," that indeed the artist simply watches as the characters "come together" and, themselves, engage in actions and difficulties. But the essay does not linger long on this point; it returns to the question of origins, declaring, still with the aid of Turgenev, that the characters simply accumulate, though to be sure the writer is "always picking them over, selecting among them"; they are so to speak "prescribed and imposed" on the artist by the life he encounters, and it is irrelevant therefore to quarrel with his subject.

Particularly the "dull dispute over the 'immoral' subject and the moral," which darkened, James said, the critical climate of his early career, seemed now "inane" from within the perspective he proceeded to establish. Significantly, the preface does not mention formulations of moral truth or wholesome principles for the guidance of conduct—the moralistic frame within which the question is argued conventionally. There too, no doubt, lay the dullness and the inanity. More significant by far is this sections' silence on the matter which the preface elsewhere makes most urgent, namely the question of the author's transactions, the question of what, if anything beyond merely picking over his store of subjects, the writer actually does. The famous paragraphs on the "moral sense of a work of art" and "the house of fiction," which together defend the writer's "boundless freedom" to take up any subject and to project "any vision," neglect anything a writer might be said to *do* and speak of him instead as a passive medium.

He is neither the sower of his story's seed nor its cultivator; he is its "soil"; the "quality and capacity" of that soil to nourish the "vision" growing there accounts for any moral quality the work may acquire. The "artist's humanity" is admittedly crucial in giving his given subject the mark of "intelligence" or "experience" which makes the work "genuine" and, moreover, gives the work its "moral sense," the "last touch of the worth of the work." Yet what that "humanity" or "sensibility" is, is a medium, whether "a rich and magnificent medium" or "a comparatively poor and ungenerous one." The moral value of the finished work, as James had stressed in his earlier studies of Baudelaire and Hawthorne, is not formulated beforehand and placed there by the writer but is an increment deriving from the richness, or poverty, of the writer's inspiration and temperament, which are part of his medium. The passage concludes by removing the discussion from the conventional language of morals and the question of the artist's intent to the terms of price and the function of form: the novel's value as a form is its "high price," its power to "preserve [its] form with closeness" while sustaining a pressure which threatens to shatter it, remaining "true to its character" only insofar as it "strains, or tends to burst, with a latent extravagance, its mould." The form and the pressure, rather than wisdom or point, are the measure of the novel's price. When the preface returns to the question of the author himself, rendering the writer as a "watcher" behind the dead walls of the house of fiction, it probes beneath the writer's actions, even the crucial act of seeing, to the sheer state of consciousness which conditions what he sees, and finally to his sheer being ("what the artist is") which accounts for the range and nature of what he is conscious of.

So complex was the process James recognized, and so circuitous, consequently, was the "long way round" the preface takes in getting to its turning point, the final account of the "grasp," the "acquisition" of Isabel

Archer. To complete the "history of the business," ascertaining what "had extraordinarily happened" to the imagination and precisely how it could "take over" the character of Isabel would in any case be "so subtle, if not so monstrous, a thing" as to be impossible. But the essay quickens as it probes further than before, and refines the question so precisely as to challenge what began as its basic assertion. The disposable figure, it now seems, was to begin with launched in movement; it was "in motion . . . , in transit"; it was certainly "bent upon its fate—some fate or other." How did the figure become so "vivid" if it were not involved in some "tangle" of conditions "to which we look for much of the impress that constitutes an identity," and if it remained in its isolation still "to be placed," since we usually account for vividness of characters "just by the business of placing them"?

The preface discovers its answer suddenly in an analogy (a "superfine" one, James felt) for the translation of life into art that recognizes the multiple expectations and contingencies which inhere in a creative process, and which, for those in the modern world, inhere in the profession of letters. It brings into focus, along with the world of affairs in Venice, the writer "picking over" his stock of subjects and *taking over* the figure of Isabel, and it presents an artist who is at once the receiving medium of his material and the manipulator of it. The image is presented in the course of acknowledging that the given character is vivid because it has already "*been* placed— placed in the imagination that detains it, preserves, protects, enjoys it, conscious of its presence in the dusky, crowded, heterogeneous back-shop of the mind very much as a wary dealer in precious odds and ends, competent to make an 'advance' on rare objects confided to him, is conscious of the rare little 'piece' left in deposit by the reduced, mysterious lady of title or the speculative amateur, and which is already there to disclose its merit afresh as soon as a key shall have clicked in a cupboard-door." The disposable figure of Isabel, accordingly, was a " 'value' " that James had, as he said, "all curiously at my disposal" in the gift shop and pawnshop of the creative mind.

The passage recalls an enterprise tangibly actual in the history of institutions and quite significant for James's conception of his office: the shop which combined a retail trade with the business of pawn, the owner serving as broker for secondhand [objets d'art and advancing money in anticipation of their sale, and acquiring items on deposit as security for small loans at high interest rates, acquiring ownership and free to sell the objects if not redeemed in a stipulated time. Its transactions—including the charity of its loans—are commercially rather than industrially productive and are sought, whether out of indigence or desperation, by individuals without routine access to the institutions of large-scale enterprise who have some pressing private need for money but no negotiable security other than their belongings. To such a shop—a curiosity shop in function, a pawnshop by prior association in James's imagination—come the Prince and Charlotte Stant in *The Golden Bowl* to look over the poetry of its contents, objects of "old gold, silver, old bronze, of old chased and jewelled artistry," its "small florid ancientries, ornaments, pendants, lockets, brooches, buckles, pretexts for dim brilliants, bloodless rubies, pearls either too large or too opaque for value . . . cups, trays, taper-stands, suggestive of pawn-tickets, archaic and brown, that would themselves, if preserved, have been prized curiosities."

In such a shop, the artist is at once a doer, a medium, and an environment or setting for what is done. He is indeed implicated in his art, though not alone by choices and preferences among his characters but by assent to the function inhering in his craft and office, his relation revealed not chiefly in the gestures of passing judgment and sentence upon characters or principles but in those of shared recognition, felt acknowledgment, or confession. The imagination, James goes on to say, is a "wary dealer," in a position to enjoy the acquisition it protects as well as to profit from the charitable transactions with the customers, including the hard-pressed lady of title or the adventuresome amateur, who placed them there. There remains the problem, however, of how to dispose of the object detained in transit, and James's wariness included the "pious desire," as he called it, "but to pace my treasure right. I quite remind myself of the dealer resigned not to 'realize,' resigned to keeping the precious object locked up indefinitely, rather than commit it, at no matter what price, to vulgar hands. For there are dealers in these forms and figures and treasures capable of that refinement.

The image of the broker is profoundly apt because it defines a suspension of multiple contingencies. It is the figure for a process rather than for the origin, simply, or the mere denouement of one. The role presented for the artist embraces the arrangements he makes and any actions he initiates, but even more important is another feature of the image: namely, that instead of emphasizing mastery of intentions, on the writer's part, or known certainties of achievement, it defines a suspension of contingent possibilities. The possibilities defined include four: that the "pious desire" might prove ineffectual and the figure be acquired and defiled to the profit of the dealer; or that the treasure in transit might remain locked up for the occasional enjoyment of the broker alone; or that a reduced lady of title, a daring amateur, might herself complete the transaction by returning to take up the form. The *Portrait* itself, as will be seen, manages to redeem all these possibilities, but the preface at hand proceeds to rephrase its statement of the writer's task: to "imagine" and "piece together" the surroundings of the figure already "bent upon its fate" and already deposited in the imagination which apprehends it, to figure out what could be the "destiny" of one among "millions of presumptuous girls" who "daily affront their destiny," this was "what one was in for—for positively organizing an ado about Isabel Archer."

The task was all the more difficult because James had welcomed the challenge of an experiment—centering the interest in the unprepossessing girl's consciousness itself rather than buttressing the " 'mere' young thing," as Shakespeare and George Eliot had done, with an entourage of equally important characters or an appropriate Romeo or Anthony. Yet, however interesting the heroine became, any shortcomings in the unbuttressed young thing would have to be compensated by the excitement of the action in order to provide fireworks for the reader's amusement. Quite suddenly, in answer to James's question "Well, what will [Isabel] do?" the agents of the fable "as if by an impulse of their own" came into view. They were the "concrete terms of [his] 'plot,' " and James's terms for his relation to them were "possession," "trust," and "contract." His actors assured him that they would show him what Isabel would do if he simply would "trust them"; James did, "with an urgent appeal to them to make it at least as interesting as they could. . . . They were like the group of attendants and entertainers who come down by train when people in the country give a party; they represented the contract for carrying the party on. That was an excellent relation with them."

James proceeded to define an equally businesslike relation with his audience: it was that of the canny servant and scrupulous employee. Dishonorable though it was, as James said, even to think of "benefits," the artist had one benefit to which he could justifiably think himself "entitled": that of "the simpler, the very simplest, forms of attention," the " 'living wage' " which the reader might be expected to pay. The more *discriminating* attention, the "finer tribute," the writer might "*enjoy*" when it came, but he could expect it only as a " 'tip,' " by taking it as a gratuity 'thrown in,' a mere miraculous windfall, the fruit of a tree he may not pretend to have shaken," a "golden apple . . . straight from the wind-stirred tree." The writer will never cease, "in wanton moods, to dream of some Paradise (for art) where the direct appeal to the intelligence might be legalized," but these dreams remain sheer "extravagances."

In speaking of himself as expecting payment but resigned to receiving only minimum wages from his audience of employers, or as expecting to be wasted and cheated by the process which fertilizes the imagination, or as resigned to foregoing profit so as to preserve a figure in his shop from desecration, or as making himself responsible, within his chosen office, for arrangements of matters which he did not initially control or possess, James acknowledged forms of experience which are shared by a number of characters in the novel but which are realized chiefly in the destiny of Isabel. But the preface also reveals other recognitions which are more unusual with brokers: that to protect, preserve, and arrange a figure in the imagination's shop was to "grasp" and possess it, for enjoyment if not for profit; that to receive "in deposit" and "take over straight from life" a figure that was placed there was to be involved in the act of placing it there in the first place; that to contract with entertainers for the "ado about Isabel" was to be in league with them and accordingly to be implicated in the action which James, though he disliked to, brought himself to name the "plot." The preface's uneasy candor in drawing attention to the novel's plot suggests the extent of James's involvement in his fiction: the watcher at the window inside the House of Fiction was also a colleague in the plot. It suggests indeed that James's fiction displays not the remote manipulations which André Gide found to be his deficiency but the very "multiplicity of his intimate connivances" which Gide demanded of the great artist. Yet, as James wrote of Turgenev, "What he thought of the relation of art to life his stories, after all, show better than anything else." In *The Portrait of a Lady,* the ploy proves to reveal the form not only of its author's mediation but of the novel's social and aesthetic implications as well.

Moreover, the plot, more clearly than other components in the novel, reveals the *Portrait*'s place in American cultural history. Far from being incidental to these historical considerations, a mere archaic artifice in a field of *realistic* techniques, moral themes, and social comment, the plot is central. And it is central also in defining the *Portrait*'s chief distinction as a literary form: its success in transforming its materials at once into movement and into visual, strictly representational, form. The novel imposes the burden of considering James's role in writing it, its place in American literature, its themes, and its representational strategy in their shared connection with the movement of the plot.

II

The Plot

If James's remarks in the preface can serve as a warning against ignoring the importance of the plot, they should warn too against reducing it to cliché oppositions of characters, abstract antitheses, or capsule summaries (Girl gets Money; American Girl marries Middle-aged Expatriate) at the cost of obscuring its very function as a form of action: its function as a relational form among events, which embraces not only motives and occasions but the full complexity of those events.

As the form of the novel's action, the plot relates to each other the main events on which the action turns: the ploy encompasses each event in its integrity (including motives of the characters but other pressures as well) while giving them together a shape and significance beyond the mere impingements of cause and effect, or linear sequences of desire and attainment, effort and failure, which would otherwise be their only connections. One of its central functions is to define the action, form being in relation to works of art what James once said it was in relation to the emotions: "the most definite thing about them." What the plot does is to connect monetary transactions with both marital and parental concerns and with aesthetic concerns as well, and to reveal a profound displacement which is of particular importance in American cultural history: a movement in which the possibilities for experience of one generation are shifted to seek their fulfillment in the prospects of a younger. In defining or shaping the limits of the action, the plot operates by inclusion but as well by exclusions, presenting each of the events which it encloses as a substitute for other possibilities which it brings to light only to postpone or exclude.

The first of these events in the novel's history is the occasion when the expatriate Mrs. Daniel Touchett, still married to her banker husband but "virtually separated from him," stops in Albany when in America on business to adopt or *take* up her niece for a trip abroad. Isabel, when her aunt unexpectedly appeared, was awaiting a call not from a surrogate parent but from her suitor, Caspar Goodwood.

The second event is the occasion when the aging banker is persuaded by his son, Ralph Touchett, to divide the son's inheritance in half so as to augment a bequest to Isabel of £5,000 to over £60,000. The father had planned to give it all to Ralph in anticipation of his marriage to Isabel; Ralph wanted, in securing this advantage for Isabel, to meet " 'the requirements of my imagination,' " having ruled out for himself a full " 'natural life' " including the possibility of marriage to Isabel, because he was dying of tuberculosis.

The third occasion occurs when the widow Madame Merle undertakes to arrange the marriage of young Isabel to Madame Merle's former lover, a forty-year-old widower, Gilbert Osmond. She hoped to " 'amuse' " and renew her former lover's interest in life, but one of her chief motives was to provide a suitable stepmother, a sizable dowry and eventually an advantageous marriage for Pansy Osmond, her illegitimate daughter whom she has never been able to acknowledge. Her project is a substitute for prospects that have proven to be impossible, including the assumption of " 'visible property' " in her own child, marriage with Osmond, or the marriage with a truly " 'great man' " that earlier had been her ambition. The prospect of Pansy's marriage, and the viability of Isabel's, are the pressing issues at the novel's end.

A fourth occasion occurs when Gilbert Osmond's sister, the Countess Gemini, discloses to Isabel the facts of Madame Merle's and Osmond's affair, Pansy's parentage, and the arrangement for Isabel's marriage. Still married to her Italian husband, but childless since the death of her own three children, she has pursued a virtually independent career in a "labyrinth of adventures." Once she had hoped that Isabel, as Osmond's wife, would triumph over him and put him in his place. Now she is moved by Isabel's deep trouble and has discovered reasons for encouraging Pansy's love for young Ned Rosier. Bored finally by her silence and by Isabel's delusion, "leaning far out" of the "window of her spirit," she tells what she knows and Isabel sits "staring at her companion's story as at a bale of fantastic wares some strolling gypsy might have unpacked . . . at her feet." Asked how she knows, she leaves Isabel with the declaration: " 'Let us assume that I've invented it!' "

The movement of the plot which shifts the ambitions and opportunities for experience from one generation to another is familiar enough in any epoch or society—part indeed of the very action of history—but one which the American imagination has characteristically found to be problematical and obsessively fascinating. The American can neither ignore the interaction of past, present, and future nor take it tranquilly for granted.

Obviously he heightens an awareness of distinctions among the generations when emphasizing the antagonisms among them—as when Jefferson, attempting to institutionalize revolution, insisted that the past was dead and that a generation's extent could and should be precisely delimited to twenty years, or when Emerson warned against enslavement to the past in The American Scholar.

But the American sharpens the distinctions among the generations even when cultivating the connections among them, the continuities of history and the patterns of tradition. One such American (Cotton Mather in the Magnalia) exhorts a lapsed generation to look backward and forward, Janus-like, in an expanding crisis, backward to the heroic fathers and exemplars whom he resurrects, forward to an unresolved but prefigured future of

"REVOLUTION" and "REFORMATION." Another (Whitman in *Democratic Vistas*) declares: "America, filling the present with greatest deeds and problems, cheerfully accepting the past, including feudalism, (as, indeed, the present is but the legitimate birth of the past, including feudalism,) counts, as I reckon, for her justification and success, (for who, as yet, dare claim success?) almost entirely on the future." More recently, a third (T. S. Eliot in "Tradition and the Individual Talent") warns against a "blind or timid adherence" to tradition, yet insists on cultivating the "consciousness of the past—not only of the pastness of the past but of its presence," counting tradition highly valuable but insisting that it "cannot be inherited" and that consequently "one must obtain it by great labour."

There is in American literature one image of this disturbed, this labored concern for history which is as grotesque and apt as the above quotations taken together: "the charming picture," as James called it, in Hawthorne's *The Dolliver Romance,* of a great-grandfather as old as Lear, cut off from "the entire confraternity of persons whom he once loved" and unable to follow them in death because he is held back by the clutched "baby-fingers" of his three-year-old great-granddaughter. The girl's name, Pansy, is echoed in *The Portrait.* More enchanting in its juxtaposition of past, present, and future is a description that is echoed in the *Portrait*'s opening setting in the "perfect middle of a splendid summer afternoon," the description of what Hawthorne found to be a typically English summer day with "positively no beginning and no end," where "Tomorrow is born before Yesterday is dead. They exist together in a golden twilight where the decrepit old day dimly discerns the face of the ominous infant; and you, though a mere mortal, may simultaneously touch them both, with one finger of recollection and another of prophecy."

James quoted this description admiringly and referred to "the charming picture of the old man and child" in the critical work on Hawthorne which he published in 1879, the year before he began work in earnest on the *Portrait.* James's immersion in the writings of Hawthorne is well known, but his *Hawthorne* proves to have a particular relevance for the *Portrait* and its plot, for Hawthorne was the one prose master of James's American predecessors to combine an obsessive interest in the past with a resolute commitment to the future. The *Portrait* itself includes echoes of Hawthorne which are rendered important by the plot, and James's published study of his master discloses not a strict model for his plot but the very matrix of its fabrication.

One echo is admittedly faint: the notice taken of an art which Madame Merle shares with Hester Prynne: her "wonderful tasks of rich embroidery . . . an art in which her bold, free invention was as noted as the agility of her needle." Another echo is stronger, however, during the important scene when Osmond and Pansy are first introduced and Madame Merle broaches her plan for Osmond's and Isabel's marriage. Osmond remarks of Pansy: " 'She's as pure as a pearl.' " Madame Merle continues: " 'Why doesn't she come back with my flowers then. . . . She doesn't like me.' " Later, it seems to Isabel that Pansy indeed might "make a perfect little pearl of a peeress." Her endowment with money and the translation of Little Pearl into a peeress is the denouement of *The Scarlet Letter*. That novel, the less famous work by John Gibson Lockart to which James compared it, and James's remarks about both underscore the importance of the *Portrait's* plot and illuminate its significance.

The Lockart novel to which James compared *The Scarlet Letter* is the *Life of Mr. Adam Blair* (1822). The burden of James's comments—he dismissed "simple resemblances and divergences of plot"—is to establish the "cold ingenious fantasy," the "passionless quality" of Hawthorne's novel about adultery in contrast to the "something warm and straight-forward" in the lesser novelist's treatment of the same subject. The paragraphs which explore the comparison, however, suggest a seminal reminiscence which owes less to the demands of the argument at hand than to the very "resemblances and divergences of plot" which a comparison of the two works brings to light. Indeed, the compulsive attraction of the comparison for James is suggested by his remark that "if one has read the two books at a short interval, it is impossible to avoid confronting them." (One slight measure of the lasting fascination for James of Lockart's book is that the names of its two principal characters, those of the wife and the widower who commit the adultery, are Charlotte and Adam, the names decades later of the adulterous wife and the widower she marries in James's *The Golden Bowl,* and that the name of Adam Blair's young wife, who dies in the first chapter, is Isabel.)

The important similarity which a comparison of the two works throws into relief is the ambivalent splicing in each of the roles of lover and parent, and the dominance finally of the institution of the family and the role of parent. (James noted that in both novels a "charming little girl" stood between the "guilty pair," and he recalled that his earliest memory of *The Scarlet Letter* [derived from a painting before he knew more than the cover of the novel] was the ineradicable image of its "two strange heroines," Hester and her daughter Pearl.) Both novels dramatize, among other things, the problematical responsibilities of parenthood, treating parenthood as a virtual mission beyond a mere physiological and perfunctory familial role, while subjecting it to the challenge of a crisis.

In Lockart's work, the Reverend Adam Blair is plunged into melan-

choly by his wife's death, when the tutelage of his little daughter Sarah
"had developed upon him." Townspeople soon begin to single out not so
much a new wife for Adam as a "step-mother" for Sarah, and one local
lady with a "motherly manner" suggests that a visit from an old friend of
Adam and Isabel, Mrs. Charlotte Campbell, would dispel Adam's gloom.
During Charlotte's stay, neighbors are struck by her "unwearied attention
to little Sarah Blair." One of the melodramatic crises of the story centers
on the daughter's fate; it occurs when Adam tries to save Sarah from
drowning, and both are rescued opportunely by Charlotte, After the se-
duction scene (in which Charlotte and liquor play the leading roles), Adam's
remorse leads him to the verge of suicide, until Charlotte checks him. Each
then acknowledges his betrayal of Adam's late wife: " 'Oh Isabel, my Saint,
my wounded Saint, my Isabel!' " and " 'sainted Isabel—thee too I have
injured—thee too have I robbed.' " Later (after Charlotte's death, Adam's
confession to his presbytery and retirement to the life of a peasant, and
finally his restoration to his congregation), Sarah turns down "many
wooers" and devotes her life to caring for her father. When he dies, twenty
years later, she retires, still unmarried, to the peasant cottage that had been
the scene of her father's "lonely life of penitence" and spends "the evening
of her days in calmness," respected by the entire parish.

In *The Scarlet Letter,* too, the role of parent is one of the first motives
introduced, in the incident when Chillingworth consents to perform a parental task, reluctantly because he is not the child's father, by administering
medicine to Pearl in the prison, and in the incident when Hester succeeds
against the magistracy (with Dimmesdale's cautious support) in keeping
Pearl in her care; indeed, the motive is established the moment that tale's
"two strange heroines" appear in the prison door. Also, Hester and
Dimmesdale, like Charlotte and Adam, are brought to acknowledge that
they have wronged the husband (though they do not call Chillingworth a
saint). Hester's lonely return to New England at the end is reminiscent of
Adam's "lonely life of penitence" and of Sarah's return, unmarried, to the
peasant cottage in the evening of her life.

Yet it is the contrasting denouements of the two novels which is most
suggestive. That of Adam Blair looks backward in tribute to Adam's memory; the parish and Scotland continue on, but no tangible future for the
community is adumbrated, and Sarah and the Blairs are cut off from any
future whatever ("With her, the race of the Blairs in that parish ended—
but not their memory."). While Sarah has virtually become a matriarch—
Adam's "only hand-maid—his only household"—without actually being
either wife or parent, and while she has virtually replaced her father in the

community's affection, her devoted care and subsequent retirement are the gestures of filial, not parental, responsibility. By contrast, *The Scarlet Letter* culminates in the adoption of parental responsibilities by all the principal adult characters, and this movement is projected ahead into an hypothetical future which is adumbrated in Hester's anticipation of "a brighter period" of history when "the whole relation between man and woman" will be founded "on a surer ground of mutual happiness," but which is prefigured more immediately and tangibly in the prospect of Little Pearl.

Under many pressures of personal motive, institutions, and circumstances, Hester first and then Dimmesdale are brought to acknowledge their passion as lovers and their responsibilities as Pearl's parents (Pearl wanders off but [remains] near at hand while they reaffirm their love in the forest, and she will accompany them in their projected escape). In Dimmesdale's case, the two roles of lover and parent are acknowledged jointly when he calls: " 'Hester . . . come hither! Come, my little Pearl' " and makes his public confession. Significantly it is Pearl's kiss, however, not Hester's, that Dimmesdale begs at the end, and Pearl's bestowal of it seals the confession and insures her development into a mature woman.

Hawthorne's "Conclusion" completes these patterns and embodies their more harmonious resolution in a prefigured future for Pearl at the cost of presenting a chapter that is too sharply detached from the body of the main novel and not fully anticipated by the movement of the story. It is nonetheless germane to its themes. Roger Chillingworth's death, along with Dimmesdale's death and Hester's self-denial at the end, underscore the novel's final emphasis on the subsequent destiny of Pearl, and moreover, their last acts authenticate and launch it. Dimmesdale's confession and his request for Pearl's embrace is matched by "the matter of business" which Hawthorne relates concerning Hester's husband. Chillingworth's last act, in a will executed at his death by the Governor and the Reverend Mr. Wilson, was virtually to adopt Pearl, administering not medicine but property by making her his heir; she becomes "the richest heiress of her day, in New England" when Chillingworth bequeaths her "a very considerable property, both here and in England." Hester's trip away with Pearl, then her separation from her to return to New England, make possible the independent adult life "in another land" which the mature Pearl is believed to enjoy. In what nation, or even on what continent, Pearl resides, the novel does not stipulate. Nor does it state whether the "armorial seals" of Pearl's letters home, with "bearings unknown to English heraldry," are more exalted in status than the "half-obliterated shield of arms" which characterized the "antique gentility" of Hester's family in Jacobean England.

The bearings may be unknown to any established heraldry or class structure whatever in the hypothetical world of Pearl's fulfillment, though they contrast distinctly with the peasant background of Adam Blair. Other features of Pearl's world, however, are more clearly prefigured. They include the monetary wealth and affection which are displayed in the presents Pearl sends her mother and the "beautiful tokens" she sews for her, in the "lavish richness of golden fancy" which Hester has indulged earlier in embroidering the letter and now in sewing garments for a grandchild who can wear them more openly in that other land, and in the marriage of Pearl, whom Hawthorne believes to be "not only alive, but married, and happy, and mindful of her mother," and herself the parent of a child.

If *Adam Blair* and *The Scarlet Letter* together define some of the main pressures that impel the plot of James's *Portrait*—patterns of marital and familial responsibility—Hawthorne's masterpiece more particularly guides its orientation. The relation between comfortable security and high status of an archaic aristocratic sort, which is suggested by Hawthorne's vocabulary but left fanciful and shadowy in Pearl's case, becomes problematic in James's novel. The "matter of business" and the role of money on which the "Conclusion" of *The Scarlet Letter* turns (and which is of genuine concern in the "Custom House" preface) are treated more emphatically by James. The place of "golden fancy," the role of the imagination, becomes more important, indeed central, in the *Portrait*. And *The Scarlet Letter*'s projection toward a resolution in a prefigured future becomes an even stronger thrust in the *Portrait,* which too confronts a future it would seek to form, though significantly it conceives that future as an urgent and unresolved crisis rather than as the hoped-for resolution of one. James's finished novel confirms what his remarks on *Adam Blair* and *The Scarlet Letter* suggest: a response to Hawthorne's novel so profound as to constitute a reworking of the earlier work's materials, a commitment of James's imagination to the fundamental impulsions which are given concrete form in Hawthorne's masterpiece.

The reworking entailed, however, one basic transformation of its materials: to bring the institution of marriage into the center of focus, to treat the "great undertaking of matrimony" as a vital and problematic form, and to mold the action around and within it, rather than to leave that institution remote in the background and dim in the future and to found the present action on alternatives to it. If James's imagination resurrected his cousin Minny Temple in creating Isabel Archer, it also brought back the Isabel who existed in name only in Lockart's novel and assigned to her as wife the burdens of tutelage, rescue, an experience which she shares with Charlotte Campbell, Hester Prynne, and later Madame Merle.

The two views of marriage that are polarized in *The Scarlet Letter* are presented also in the *Portrait:* the sheerly conventional marriage figured in the failure of Hester and Chillingworth (their marriage the emptiest of conventions, their relation now a shadowy perfunctory marriage still recognized but buried in secrecy and in the past, without foundation in behavior or desire) and the marriage posited for Pearl, marriage as a form of fruition and aspiration. But in James's work they are manifest in many and complex versions which render their extremes less patently antagonistic. Marriage as a hollow factitious form—viewed at one point in the *Portrait* as the " 'ghastly form' "—and marriage as a form of fulfillment and creative possibilities—called at one point "the magnificent form"—are more intimately and problematically related. Indeed, one of the creative functions of the plot is to constitute this close relation between the two by splicing together the immediate plan for Isabel's marriage and the more long-range provisions, still unsettled at the novel's end, for Pansy's. The splicing is strengthened by the fact that Isabel and Pansy attract common suitors. Lord Warburton, whose proposal Isabel turns down, is latter an unsuccessful suitor of Pansy. And the younger Ned Rosier, who loves Pansy and whom Pansy would like to marry, had been at the age of twelve a childhood acquaintance, an "angelic" infatuation, of Isabel.

James's plot accordingly enabled him to solve a technical problem that Hawthorne handled less satisfactorily (the structural relation between the bulk of the work and its conclusion, between the destiny of Hester, Dimmesdale, and Chillingworth and that of Pearl) and to mediate more successfully the shift from the older generation's opportunities to the younger's that his novel helps to make a burden and a mission for American culture. The process by which the plot orients the novel's movement, drawing the characters into the action it shapes while delineating their characters, is displayed in the amplitude of character, imagery, and incident of the *Portrait* itself.

III

The Marriage

The first of the important characters to be engaged by the plot and implicated in its moral consequences are those who initiate it and display the main outline of its significance, the interconnection of marital and familial, monetary, and aesthetic concerns: the older Touchetts, Daniel and

Lydia, still linked but no longer intimate in their "experiment in matrimony." They find awakened interest, and Mrs. Touchett finds convenience as a hostess, in the niece they have taken up and are supporting while diverting her from the dry sands of German philosophy to a more direct exposure to Europe and the past. It is Mrs. Touchett's telegram (she has mastered " 'the art of condensation' ") that announces in chapter 1 that she has " 'Taken sister's girl' " and that Isabel is soon to arrive at Gardencourt. Touchett himself, with his earned and banked resources, long ago bought a house, which imaged all English history since Edward VI, for the simple reason that it was "a great bargain." But as a consequence of this purchase he now has it in his "careful keeping" and has acquired "a real aesthetic passion" for his Gardencourt. He stands firm against the aimless boredom, the jocular detachment, of his son and his son's friend, Lord Warburton, and has suggested that Warburton " 'take hold' of something"—indeed marry an interesting woman so that his " 'life will be more interesting,' " though he jokingly excludes the niece of whose impending arrival he has just heard. Later, in his bequest to Isabel, he deliberately consents to play along with his son's plan to make Isabel rich although he fears it risky to the point of being irresponsible, even " 'immoral.' "

That plan, if immoral, is also creative. Ralph Touchett's plan is founded on renouncing prospects of marriage with Isabel and on translating his affection into something paternal and fraternal instead. And it is founded on actions in which *both* the renunciation and the use of his inherited wealth are fused. If he is, as one character claims, " 'Prospero enough to make [Isabel] what she has become,' " he is nonetheless like the plotter Iago in wanting to " 'put money in her purse.' " He wants to put money in her purse so that he might, and she might, "meet the requirements of their imagination." With his permissive and playful imagination, he has, as he remarks, " 'amused myself with planning out a high destiny for you' " and after her disastrous marriage to Osmond he spends what time he can watching her, entertained in trying to see through the mask of tranquil satisfaction she has assumed. He presses the limits of their "tacit convention" not to discuss Osmond's conduct openly, for he is so involved in her predicament that he feels "an almost savage desire to hear her complain of her husband," longing "for his own satisfaction more than for hers" to show that he understood her situation, trying again and again "to make her betray Osmond" though "he felt cold-blooded, cruel, dishonourable almost, in doing so." He is turning about in pained fascination the figure detained in the imagination's shop. It is an anguished entertainment, founded on money and imagination, love and sacrifice, and when Isabel later disobeys her husband to rush to Ralph's deathbed, his affection for his cousin becomes adoration in his final declaration.

Unlike Ralph, who has renounced the prospect of marriage, his friend Lord Warburton, young Ned Rosier, and Caspar Goodwood find their place as suitors in the novel's action. Warburton exerts a definite but ambivalent charm throughout the novel. He pursues an active career in Parliament and is a "nobleman of the newest pattern" for he combines the security of his wealth and station with the programs of the " 'radicals of the upperclass' " who, in Daniel Touchett's view, indulge in their theories as a luxuriously safe " 'amusement' " without profound commitment. Isabel continues to like Warburton's manliness and all "his merits—properties these partaking of the essence of great decent houses, as one might put it." When he proposes to her she feels "that a territorial, a political, a social magnate had conceived the design of drawing her into" his "system," though she recognized that in his genuine tact and decency he was "looking at her with eyes charged with the light of a passion that had sifted itself clear of the baser parts of emotion—the heat, the violence, the unreason. . . ." Though he insists that he simply offers her " 'the chance of taking the common lot in a comfortable way' " she declines his "big bribe" on the grounds that she cannot detach herself from " 'the common lot,' "— from the " 'usual chances and dangers, from what most people know and suffer,' "—that, as she says, " 'I can't escape my fate.' "

His presence becomes more disturbing in the later part of the novel; at the age of forty-two he has become Pansy's suitor, and Madame Merle and Osmond find him the answer to their ambitions for Pansy, and Osmond demands that Isabel encourage the match. Though Isabel finds Warburton's friendship a comfort—"it was like having a large balance at the bank"—it becomes problematical because there are definite grounds for the suspicion Ralph and the Countess Gemini share: that a large part of Warburton's interest in Pansy is the desire to be near her stepmother. There is a complicated emotional involvement beneath the oddity, as Osmond puts it to Isabel, that " 'Pansy's admirers should all be your old friends.' " Isabel displays more interest in Warburton's robust masculinity than she did earlier, noticing now how Pansy gives "quiet oblique glances at his person, his hands, his feet, his clothes," how Pansy's "eyes, as usual, wandered up and down his robust person as if he had offered it to her for exhibition." These are the observations of a vicarious participant.

Warburton and Isabel tacitly recognize this involvement on one occasion when Isabel "met his eyes, and for a moment they looked straight at each other," and this recognition simply tightens her dilemma, for the plot has created a situation which complicates the relation between her roles as wife and parent and her relation with her former suitor: to obey her husband's demand by encouraging Warburton's courtship of Pansy would prove that she did not fear Warburton's presence but risk making her relation to him more intimate; to disobey her husband out of concern for Pansy's feelings by encouraging Pansy's favorite, Ned Rosier, would safeguard her conduct from emotional complications with Warburton but virtually acknowledge that she fears Warburton's proximity and envies Pansy his affection. She assures Warburton he may court Pansy if he pleases, but instantly afterward promises Ned to " 'do what I can' " to favor his suit; yet even after Pansy confesses her love for the younger man, Isabel does not speak in his favor but speaks, albeit without force, of Pansy's obligation to respect her father's desire and of the importance of Warburton's title and fortune.

The crisis is not resolved by Isabel but by a decision of Warburton which is in keeping with the basic design of the plot. He withdraws without making a proposal, understanding Isabel's predicament and recognizing that the younger girl is not in love with him. Later when Isabel learns that Warburton, after a courtship of three weeks, has married " 'A member of the aristocracy; Lady Flora, Lady Felicia—something of that sort,' " she reflects that Warburton "was dead for poor Pansy; by Pansy he might have lived." But instead of becoming the perfect little pearl of a peeress, Pansy will wait in hopes of marrying Ned who looks to her so like a "nobleman."

Before Pansy's prospects and Isabel's concern turn from Warburton to the young man, Ned Rosier's place in the action seems inconsequential, for there is justice in Isabel's feeling that Ned is "really so light a weight. He was much more of the type of the useless fine gentleman than the English nobleman," and Warburton is probably not envious in remarking that Ned still " 'doesn't look much more than twelve today.' " He is an American expatriate and dilettante (" 'There's nothing for a gentleman in America' "). And he lacks not only Warburton's title but a career (" 'American diplomacy—that's not for gentlemen either' "), and instead of Warburton's radical views he has the "grim politics," reactionary and Napoleonic, which he parrots (prophetic soul) from one Mr. Luce. Yet for all the novel's frivolous attention to the decorations of his mantelpiece, his prominent position in the plot suggests his importance, for he is carefully introduced just after Madame Merle learns that Isabel has inherited a fortune, and his arrival in Rome is the first narrated incident to follow Isabel's marriage. With his "cultivated tastes" and collection of bibelots, he all but lives at the auctioneer's, yet he could not possibly have a career as shopkeeper because, as he says, " 'I can buy very well, but I can't sell.' " In the course of the novel, however, he has found temporarily a place in the world of affairs. He has been drawn into the final crisis by paying court to Pansy and rendering himself eligible by the commercial transaction which he announces to Isabel when he finds her seated in the "despoiled arena" of the Coliseum: he has sold his *objets d'art* (all but his enamels) for $50,000 cash.

Ned's relation with Isabel spans the years from their childhood to a point which lies beyond the range of her personal desire, but the relation of Caspar Goodwood is at once more confined and more intimate. The first suitor to propose to Isabel (in Albany), he is the last to confront her in the novel, when he tries to persuade her to leave her husband. With his square jaw and the "hardness of presence, in his way of rising before her" that Isabel finds disagreeable, his manner presents a distinct combination of masculine vigor and the awkward and genuine assertiveness of the American businessman. Isabel is critical of the sameness of his apparel, the simplicity of his manner, and later his literalness, and she early compares the prospect of "conquest at her English suitor's [Warburton's] large quiet hands" to the more unsettling prospect of letting Caspar "take positive possession of her." He manages a large cotton mill in Massachusetts and is the son of its founder; his business acumen, energy, and career distinguish him from both Warburton and Rosier. So complete is his association with the realm of business that in a later scene with Isabel, when restating his love for her and trying to understand her distance from him, his very idiom makes the world of business the dividing line between himself and the intimacy of Isabel's feelings: the phrase "none of my business" becomes a virtual refrain as he concedes, time and again, that " 'It's none of my business—very true. But I love you.' "

Yet within the novel's perspective her feelings are related, curiously, to his business, for his business capacity includes the "sharp eye" that has already led him to one patented invention and it includes "the art," as James said, "of managing men." Two statements which James added in revision enforce Goodwood's connection with the plot and the artistry of making it: in his "clear-burning eyes" sits "some watcher at a window," and he is expected someday to "write himself in bigger letters." It is he, Isabel expects, who will see through her mask if anyone can and "make . . . out, as over a falsified balance-sheet . . . the intimate disarray of her affairs." He had "invested his all in her happiness, while the others had invested only a part." The plot renders these scattered metaphors central, rather than peripheral or incidental, to the novel's design. By the final chapter, when Caspar's strong desire is buttressed by Ralph's last request to " 'Do everything you can for her; do everything she'll let you,' " Caspar's "aimless, fruitless passion" has become profound and possessive, and the plot has made of him an image of a grasping and possessive imagination.

The plot's chief instruments and artificers, however, are those who give the confluence of events its distinct shape: Madame Merle and her former lover, Gilbert Osmond. With one marriage a failure, others are seemingly out of the question for Serena Merle, and she finds it impossible to acknowledge Pansy Osmond as her daughter. She conceives the simultaneous arrangement of Isabel's marriage and the provision eventually for Pansy's, hoping to " 'amuse' " her former lover and urging him to " 'profit' " by her deep familiarity with social arrangements. She is an expatriate, so steeped now in " 'the old, old world' " as to be " 'the great round world itself.' " Madame Merle seems to be deeply conventional in a world where the conventional touches upon everything, including, as Isabel recognizes, language itself. Not only does Madame Merle practice the arts of conversation and the needle, to say nothing of music, but she paints: she "made no more of brushing in a sketch than of pulling off her gloves." Isabel's partial awakening to the facts of her betrayal include the recognition (which the preface was to echo later) that Madame Merle had been a powerful "agent" in her "destiny."

Indeed, she has done for James what the Countess Gemini finally divulges that she has done for Osmond: " 'She has worked for him, plotted for him, suffered for him; she has even more than once found money for him.' " Her plotting, once it is revealed, not only calls forth Isabel's scorn but her compassion when she recognizes that Madame Merle has, as the Countess says, " 'failed so dreadfully that she's determined her daughter shall make it up.' " Her own ambitions and desires, like Isabel's are channeled, by the plot she does so much to instigate, into the prospects for Pansy's marriage. Her final failure is to be excluded even as a silent partner from the arrangements she had wanted so much to be " 'my work' " by Osmond who abandons her.

It is Osmond who is stirred to a renewed interest in life by collaboration in his colleagues's plot. An "odd mixture of the detached and involved," living by himself in a "sifted, arranged world" in Italy, "thinking about art and beauty and history," This proud " 'provincial' " is an American expatriate artist and dilettante. He longs nostalgically for the authority of a pope and suggests occasionally in his demeanor a "prince in exile," a " 'prince who has abdicated in a fit of fastidiousness and has been in a state of disgust ever since.' " He is the incarnation of taste and, as he himself puts it, " 'convention itself.' " He had once had the decency to acknowledge his own daughter Pansy and, unlike Madame Merle's husband who rejected the child utterly, to make himself responsible for her care; during his engagement to Isabel he suggests that together they will "make up some little life" for Pansy, as if they were to invent it; late in the novel, "playing theoretic tricks on the delicate organism of his daughter," and wanting to "show that if he regarded his daughter as a precious work of art it was natural he should be more careful about the finishing touches," he sends her back to the Roman convent to insure her complete subservience to his will.

He is imaged as a commemorative "gold coin" and is discovered late in the novel devoting his art to copying an illustration of an "antique coin," scorning money but using ant seeking it. His old villa in Florence—"a blank-looking structure," broken by only "a few windows," its front facade the "mask" rather than the "face of the house"—harbors inside a large "writing-table of which the ingenious perfection bore the stamp" not of Renaissance Florence but of "London and the nineteenth century." There lives the man "with eyes at once vague and penetrating . . . expressive of the observer as well as of the dreamer," to whose "deep art" Isabel eventually succumbs. If he discreetly seeks public approval, looking "out of his window even when he appeared to be most detached from it" so as to gain its recognition rather than to "enlighten or convert or redeem it," he is also the watcher inside their common dwelling whom Isabel recognizes in her long night of meditation—the watcher who "seemed to peep down from a small high window and mock at her." "Her mind," she comes to understand, "was to be his. . . . He would rake the soil gently and water the flowers. . . . It would be a pretty piece of property for a proprietor already far reaching." He is the figure—the watcher inside the House of Fiction—in whom Caspar recognizes much later a "demonic imagination."

So intimately is James implicated in the action of his novel that letters he was writing while working on the *Portrait* are echoed in the passages where Osmond's mind and feelings are stirred by the workings of the plot and he proposes marriage to Isabel. James wrote that he was "much more interested in my current work than anything else," that he was "working with great ease, relish, and success," that his work would bring $6,000 from serialization alone, that it would "rend the veil" which covered his "ferocious ambition," that it would be from the finished *Portrait*, his most ambitious early effort, "that I myself shall pretend to date." It is Ralph who notices that the costumed "fine lady" which the once "free, keen" Isabel has become "represented Gilbert Osmond," who now "was in his element; at last he had material to work with." His calculated effects "were produced by no vulgar means, but the motive was as vulgar as the art was great. . . . 'He works with superior material,' Ralph said to himself; 'it's rich abundance compared with his former resources.' " It is the excitement of such opportunities that earlier had awakened Osmond. Just before his proposal Osmond finds himself pleased with his newly aroused "sense of success," feeling that his earlier successes had rested "on vague laurels," and that his present success was "easy . . . only because he had made an altogether exceptional effort." While the "desire to have something or other to show for his 'parts' . . . had been the dream of his youth," now it was to materialize with Isabel's help and at her expense: "If an anonymous drawing on a museum wall had been conscious and watchful it might have known this peculiar pleasure of being at last . . . identified—as from the hand of a great master—by the so high and so unnoticed fact of style. His 'style' is what the girl had discovered with a little help; and now, beside herself enjoying it, she should publish it to the world without his having any of the trouble. She would do the thing for him and he would not have waited in vain." In this view of Osmond are joined both the finished work of art—the drawing with which Osmond is associated so intimately—and the master whose style was displayed in making it.

The useful girl is Isabel with her combination of caution and curiosity, inexperience and alertness, and the strength of will which leads her to confront life's options " 'So as to choose.' " Her suspicion of the poisoned cup of experience and her fear of suffering are countered by her desire to join in what ordinary " 'people know and suffer.' " Her desire "to leave the past behind her" and encounter always fresh beginnings is balanced by her deepening response to the appeal of the past and tradition. Her acknowledged ignorance "about bills" or " 'anything about money' " is countered by the definiteness of her aversion " 'to being under pecuniary obligations' " and the assurance of her delusion that in going to Europe she is literally " 'travelling at her own expense.' " The "something cold and dry in her temperament" which an "unappreciated suitor" would notice is countered by the boldness of her "ridiculously active imagination which renders her vulnerable to delusions, being so "wide-eyed" as to suffer from "seeing too many things at once" and incurring the "penalty of having given undue encouragement to the faculty of seeing without judging." Her mind in sum is a "tangle of vague outlines at the start," but the interaction of her capacity for experience with the plot which forms that experience joins her conscience and her imagination and fills in the outlines of both Isabel's and the *Portrait*'s vision.

In the course of experiencing the lures and pressures that shape her destiny in the novel, the action brings her maternal instincts into the foreground. Mrs. Touchett's taunting fear that Isabel may decide that her " 'mission in life's to prove that a stepmother may sacrifice herself—and that, to prove it, she must first become one' " is confirmed by Isabel's feeling toward Pansy and by her eventual actions, and it is given another dimension by Isabel's late recognition that her feeling for Osmond himself contained "a maternal strain—the happiness of a woman who felt that she was a contributor, that she came with charged hands."

Moreover, the plotted action which involves her with Osmond and Pansy dissociates both Isabel and finally Pansy from the securities and settled conventions of the strictly aristocratic tradition, embodied in Lord Warburton, and involves each instead in something more problematical and hazardous. For Pansy it is the prospect of a marriage founded on no more than sheer mutual affection and a great sufficiency of cash; Pansy herself, whom Isabel feels to be a blank page she hopes will be filled with "an edifying text," displays nothing but her fragile charm and the genuineness of her devotion; Ned Rosier has neither settled status nor job and office, his mind and tastes are not exceptional, and his only recommendation is the genuine commitment defined by his courtship and the sale of his prized treasures.

Isabel's involvement is with the actual form of her strange marriage with Osmond. Within that form Isabel's and Osmond's child is born (he dies at the age of six months) and Isabel acquires her stepdaughter. Within a few years, however, it is clear that intimacy between Isabel and Osmond has ceased, and by the end his attitude is one of contempt; as Isabel finally tells him, " 'It's malignant.' " Yet the form, as a sheer institutional form, still holds and within it takes place a striking confrontation when Isabel distinguishes between her own and her husband's conceptions of aristocracy and tradition. It is not only striking but significant because their different attitudes together reveal conflicting tendencies that are widespread in American culture but which are particularly pressing in the Genteel Tradition, and these tendencies are embodied in the marriage which the plot has figured for them.

Isabel's view of aristocracy is distinguished by being ethical and experiential and envisions the reconciliation of duty with enjoyment: the "union of great knowledge with great liberty; the knowledge would give one a sense of duty and the liberty a sense of enjoyment." Osmond's is at once more formal and more active; it is "altogether a thing of forms, a conscious, calculated attitude." And while both characters respect tradition, the "old, the consecrated, the transmitted," and both speak is if dissociated from it and encountering it from some distance, Isabel's attitude is eclectic and based on her determination "to do what she chose with it." Osmond's view is at once more conservative in its deference to older social patterns, more desperate in his sense of alienation from them, and more radical in his means to attain them, as befits the prince in exile from America and would-be pope who longs for the deference paid an aristocrat but has not inherited the traditional aristocratic forms. He has a "large collection" of traditions and feels that the "great thing was to act in accordance with them" rather than to choose among them; and his proprietorship, like his manner, is founded on the realization that distinguishes him from the European who could simply find or tranquilly inherit his traditions: Osmond, the American expatriate, knows that "if one was so fortunate as not to have [tradition] one must immediately proceed to make it."

Isabel's determination to "choose," and Osmond's to construct or "make," are sharply delineated by the mutual antagonism of the two characters, but they are joined in perilous proximity by the bond of their marriage and both are related to other social realities which are part of their American background. These are the money economy and obsessive attitudes toward money, which characterize the culture of American capitalism, and characteristic American attitudes (one utilitarian, the other guilt-ridden) toward inherited wealth.

Osmond, the son of a "rich and wild" father and a mother who combined a practical "administrative" view with a talent for poor poetry, has made in his expatriation a " 'willful renunciation' " which is nonetheless a social construct; it is founded on the habitual intent to utilize economic resources without creating them and is centered on his immediate family. Determined " 'not to strive nor struggle' " in the business world, yet content with the independent income derived therefrom (though he thinks it " 'little' "), he carefully harbors and manages his economic resources, buys and builds his collection and refines his tastes, buys and constructs his walled substitute for a world of forms which he might prefer to have inherited. Making his " 'life an art' " as he advised Isabel to do, he attempts to mold Pansy, with his "artistic" or "plastic view" of her capacities, in accordance with his desire for dominance. He is the genteel embodiment of "convention" in a strikingly modern version recognizable since 1789: convention become conscious and deliberate, the result less of habit and tacit agreement than of calculated control, deliberate formulation, and the determination not simply to order life as it is but to shape it more firmly and actually change it. When the opportunity to gain Isabel and her fortune presents itself, he is happy for the opportunity to put it and her to use.

Isabel and her fortune come to be as closely associated in her own mind as they are in Osmond's and as they are throughout the novel. In chapter 1, Ralph Touchett, after reading the reference in his mother's telegram to Isabel's being " 'independent,' " asks this question: is the word " 'used in a moral or in a financial sense?' " His question proves to have point. After Isabel has accustomed herself to the fact that she is rich, she is enchanted by a "maze of visions" of what a generous, independent, responsible girl could do with such resources, and her fortune "became to her mind a part of her better self; it gave her importance, gave her even, to her own imagination, a certain ideal beauty." Her attitude has less conscious origins in her temperament and in her environment, the attitudes toward experience and money being so intimate that the novel renders the one the image of the other. When Osmond proposes, Isabel is checked by a sense of dread, her hesitancy being founded on "the force which . . . ought to have banished all dread—the sense of something within herself, deep down, that she supposed to be inspired and trustful passion." Yet that fount of passion is one which Isabel inclines to save as against the alternative she anticipates, that of spending it entirely: "It was there like a large sum stored in a bank—which there was a terror in having to begin to spend. If she touched it, it would all come out." (This analogy between a bank and Isabel's capacity for passion was added in revision.) By the time she is engaged, her consent is taking the form of an act of absolution and benefaction but also of proprietorship.

She is gratified by Pansy's affection, for "Pansy already so represented part of the service she should render," and if she feels "humility" in surrendering to Osmond, she feels also "a kind of pride," in the knowledge that "she should be able to be of use to him" and that "she was not only taking, she was giving." When Isabel looks back on her decision later, she recognizes that she never would have married him "but for her money." Her money had been the contribution to the marriage that appealed to her "maternal strain," yet the indelicacy of having merely inherited it was also a "burden" on her conscience which she longed to transfer to someone else. "What would lighten her own conscience more effectually than to make it over to the man with the best taste in the world" when she could think of no charitable institution as interesting as he? "He would use her fortune in a way that would make her think better of it and rub off a certain grossness attaching to the good luck of an unexpected inheritance." Moreover, she had felt that the "subtlest . . . manly organism she had ever known had become her property, and the recognition of having but to put out her hands and take it had been originally a sort of act of devotion."

These divergent views—of proprietorship, the propriety of money,

domestic economy, parental care, tradition, and aristocratic forms and values—are held juxtaposed within the bond of Isabel's and Osmond's marriage. Their variety, their tension, and their proximity are an indication
that not only the separate views themselves but their interconnections are
being examined, and that the form which joins them, the marriage, is being
subjected to a test under the pressures shaped by the plot. Indeed, the
marriage institution as displayed is not a settled institutional mold but is a
form in the process of being shaped. The terms "experiment" for the
Touchetts' marriage and "undertaking" for matrimony in general are decidedly apt in the context of the *Portrait*—and with them the term "form,"
which is used by Caspar when condemning the " 'ghastly form' " which
Isabel's marriage has become and is used also when Osmond, urging Isabel
not to leave, is said to speak "in the name of something sacred and precious—the observance of a magnificent form."

For the *Portrait* reveals in the institution the principal functions of a
form: the capacity to sustain a fully developed relationship; but also the
capacity to precede the full development of a process or experience while
yet prefiguring it, and thus to shape the plans and aspirations for personal
and social experience, to embody emerging possibilities as well as actual
achievements; and the capacity to survive the process or experience itself,
remaining a skeletal but nonetheless real image of possibilities not longer
(or not yet again) actual. Within the context of the *Portrait,* the marriages
of the Countess and much later of Warburton image the institution reduced
to its most factitiously conventional status, while Daniel Touchett's hopes
for Ralph's and Isabel's marriage, and earlier for Warburton's, and Isabel's
hopes for Pansy's, view the institution as a form of aspiration and commitment, with the Touchetts' marriage (and Henrietta Stackpole's) falling
in between.

Indeed, the *Portrait* gives body to ambivalent remarks James made in
letters to his brother and Grace Norton, in 1878 and 1881, on the subject
of marriage, confirming his intention not to marry but insisting on the
importance of the institution, associating the form of marriage with commitments of the profoundest sort, and displaying a firm regard for the
institution despite his own decision. He wrote that "I believe almost as
much in matrimony for most other people as I believe in it little for myself,"
and that "one's attitude toward marriage is . . . the most characteristic part
doubtless of one's general attitude toward life. . . . If I were to marry I
should be guilty in my own eyes of inconsistency—I should pretend to
think quite a bit better of life than I really do." These letters make the form
of marriage an image of commitments to life itself, whether within or

beyond the range of one's actual conduct. These are commitments which James's imagination entertained and made in his fiction, if nowhere else, and they are at issue in the *Portrait*.

There the plot—like the world it represents endowing and then drawing on Isabel's banked resources of temperament and inheritance—focuses first on the prospective form of her marriage; then as that becomes a hollow shell it widens its focus to include the prospects for Pansy's. In the process, Isabel's acts of confronting and imagining experience become acts of paying and suffering and responsible commitment as she is led by her husband "into the mansion of his own habitation" and made a victim of her world (including her own temperament and illusions) and of the *Portrait* which creates and paints her.

Revision and Thematic Change in *The Portrait of a Lady*

Nina Baym

When Henry James revised *The Portrait of a Lady* for the New York edition he made thousands of changes in the wording of the text. (*The Portrait of a Lady* was originally serialized in twelve installments in *Macmillan's Magazine* beginning in October 1880 and in the *Atlantic Monthly* beginning one month later. First editions were separately published in England and America in 1881. The first edition shows a few hundred minor revisions in wording from the serialized version. The New York edition, a selection of James's writing, appeared from 1907 to 1909, the extensively reworded text of *The Portrait* being published in 1908.) The revised version is stylistically and thematically closer to his later interests than the early one had been. Its writing is more complex, mannered, and metaphorical. It is thematically less timely and realistic, for its main concern is the private consciousness. In the 1908 version, Isabel Archer's inner life is the center of the character and of the novel's reality. In the early version the inner life is only one aspect of character, which is defined by behavior in a social context.

Owing to the prestige of the New York edition, the novel of 1881 has largely been ignored by readers and critics, with a resulting loss in our sense of the early James as opposed to the later. In particular we do not see how topical and timely *The Portrait of a Lady* was. The 1881 novel was one of an increasing number of works about "the woman question." The heroine, an appealing young American, wants to live an independent and meaningful life; but she is thwarted. Unlike many works of the period on

From *Modern Fiction Studies* 22, no. 2 (Summer 1976). © 1976 by the Purdue Research Foundation, West Lafayette, Indiana.

this theme, *The Portrait* did not depict Isabel's desire as unnatural and mis-guidedly unfeminine, nor did it employ the standard formula of saving her from this delusion by love and marriage. On the contrary, the novel sym-pathized with her aim to the point of calling both love and marriage into question. Moreover, it judged Isabel as limited by those inner qualities that, together with external obstacles, prevented her from pursuing and realizing her wish.

The changes of 1908, transforming the story into a drama of con-sciousness, overlaid and in places obliterated the coherence of the 1881 version. Omissions and additions altered all the characters significantly. Finally, James wrote a preface for the new work which announced that the story centered in the heroine's consciousness and that its action was the development of her perception and awareness. The preface instructed the reader in how to interpret, what to admire, and what to deplore in the work. This preface is significant because it has largely controlled the critical readings of *The Portrait*. Since its interpretation works for 1908 but not so well for 1881, readers turning to the early version with the preface in mind naturally find an imperfect approximation of the revision. In case after case, passages which figure importantly in criticism of *The Portrait* occur in 1908 only. Strong arguments for Isabel's spiritual transcendence, and equally strong arguments for her hypocritical egotism, derive from that text. But the version of 1881 is a different work. Early James was a masterful writer with his own interests. Once recovered, the 1881 story with its topical focus on the "new woman" and its skillful use of fictional formulae, may prove to be just as interesting as the version of 1908.

The most extensive revisions concern Isabel Archer. She appears on almost every page of the book, and virtually every page about her undergoes change. Although some of these are only excisions or substitutions of single words, the cumulative effect is considerable. The chief intent of these changes is to endow her with the acute, subtle consciousness required for a late James work, which the early Isabel lacks. At the same time that James gives her a rich mental life in 1908, he effaces the original main quality of her character, emotional responsiveness. Her intellectual agility is greatly extended at the expense of her emotional nature.

From this basic change, others follow. Early Isabel is trapped by her simplicity; late Isabel must be the dupe of her subtlety. Victimized by an appeal to her highest faculties, she is less a fool than a saint. There is a corresponding change of tone to treat this more remarkable being. For example, "brilliant and noble" in 1881 becomes "high and splendid . . . and yet oh so radiantly gentle!" in 1908, while "a bright spirit" is rewritten as "a 'lustre' beyond any recorded losing or rediscovering" (chap. 37). As Isabel is exalted, other characters are degraded. Madame Merle and Osmond are thoroughly blackened, and many supporting figures are flattened and undercut by exaggerated comic treatment. The change in the two villains enhances the pathos in the situation of the trapped sensibility—Isabel Archer as redrawn is much more like Milly Theale than like the original Isabel Archer—while the minor characters lose their function as independent centers of judgment and awareness in the novel. When he is through, James has left nothing solid for the reader except the boundless imagination of Isabel. But in 1881 a limited imagination is her greatest shortcoming.

In 1881, Isabel is an intelligent, sensitive, perceptive, idealistic girl with a ready interest in life. Her imagination, however is conventionally romantic (like that of many other heroines of fiction), the natural expression of a youthful spirit limited in education and experience. Unfortunately, this imaginativeness is mistaken by Isabel and those who surround her as some sort of brilliance. Isabel's overestimation of herself is a fault, but her real wish to be morally and spiritually fine is extremely attractive. Endowing her with a real, rather than a fancied, imaginative superiority in 1908, James takes away the aspiring quality of her character which is so endearing. Making her live intensely in her mind rather than her feelings, he deprives her of some of the appealing spontaneity, vivacity, and activity in the 1881 character.

Let us note some of the changes which make her more observant and less active, more intellectual and less emotional. In chapter 2, "quick" perception becomes "clear," "startled" eyes merely "widen," and "brilliant" eyes are toned down to "lighted." In chapter 3, Isabel finds the rainy springtime "a questionable improvement" over winter; this is sophisticated in 1908 to "an appeal—and it seemed a cynical, insincere appeal—to patience," just as "the incongruities of the season" become "cosmic treacheries." "Fresh impressions" of her "entertaining" Aunt Lydia become "a matter of high but easy irony, or comedy," which "so held" her, and Mrs. Touchett's "deeply interesting" conversation changes to "food for deep reflexion." Vague impulses of feeling are replaced by more precise thoughts, and ordinary ideas become more intense and extravagant.

This process continues even in indirect changes like the alteration of Isabel's wish not to "take a nap" in 1881 to a disinclination for "dozing forgetfulness" in 1908. Taking a nap is a simple physical action; dozing forgetfulness shows that for Isabel sleep means a sacrifice of intellectual activity. In the same chapter (chap. 4) Isabel's "heart" is changed to her "soul" and her having "gone so far as to forgive" becomes "committed the conscious solecism of forgiving." Similarly, "a certain feeling of embarrassment" becomes "a new sense of complications." The emotion of uneasiness is regularly replaced in 1908 by this sense of complication; another example occurs in chapter 27 when Lord Warburton's appearance in the first version "made her vaguely uneasy" but in 1908 "affected her as a complication of the wrong sort—she liked so complications of the right." In chapter 6, James removes the characterizing word "impulsively," and revises "absorbing happiness" to "fine, full consciousness" and "artless" to "prompt." In chapter 9, he replaces "coquetry" with "the calculation of her effect" and in chapter 11 "a fine freedom of composition" with "a free play of intelligence." James is recreating the heroine as a person who is continually "reading" her environment and is consequently less active in it.

James brings this out clearly in changing her responses toward her suitors from feeling and impulse to reflection and analysis. She judges their offers in 1908 according to whether life with them will support imaginative freedom. Visions of a "completed life" with Lord Warburton in 1881 change to "completed consciousness" in 1908; instead of possibly being "an incumbrance" Lord Warburton may represent "a complication of every hour"; an offer that "failed to correspond to any vision of happiness" in 1881 "failed to support any enlightened prejudice in favour of the free exploration of life" in 1908; and "elements that would displease her" became "narrowing elements . . . a stupefying anodyne" (chap. 12). As for Caspar Goodwood, his "limitations" became "impediments to the finer respiration" (chap. 21). Isabel in 1881 is much more ordinary, so to speak, in that she wants happiness and pleasure from a relationship with a man; in 1908, her requirements are more ascetic and aesthetic.

James also rewrote passages describing her responses to Europe. Her "impressions" change to a "fulness" of "response" and her "feelings" of Rome predictably become her "consciousness" of the city. St. Peter's is no longer just a "church" to her, but "the greatest of human temples" (chap. 27). In this context, the image of Osmond on his hilltop (chap. 26) which "happened to take her fancy particularly" in 1881 is revised in 1908 to "put on for her a particular harmony with other supposed and divined things, histories within histories." Isabel's awareness replaces her faculty of feeling in 1908; she responds with her mind rather than her emotions. In 1881 Isabel's emotions, besides being quick, are also rather imprecise. The 1908 responses are more intellectual and also more specific. But imprecision in 1881 is not a stylistic fault; it conveys an important aspect of Isabel's character. She respects herself partly as a person of sensibility, and rightly so, but the vagueness of her feelings leads directly to many of her mistakes. (James tells us all this in the long analytic passages of chapter 6, but much of what he says no longer seems applicable in 1908.) Because she values her feelings she permits, even encourages, them to guide her. But good and true feelings can be as treacherous as bad ones. This point is important for the theme of *The Portrait* in 1881 and for James's handling of Isabel in love. Love is necessarily quite different in the two versions. In 1881 James makes Isabel genuinely in love with Osmond, shows that this real feeling is untrustworthy, and demonstrates thereby how the desire for independence can be subverted by true love.

In 1908, love is complicated by the heroine's self-awareness. She is not a character likely to get swept away on a wave of feeling. The question of her attraction to Osmond is a major interpretive problem in the 1908 version. One example will demonstrate the nature of James's changes. In 1881, when Osmond declares his love, Isabel feels dread. "What made her dread great was precisely the force which, as it would seem, ought to have banished all dread—the consciousness of what was in her own heart. It was terrible to have to surrender herself to that" (chap. 29). Here is a conventional maidenly response to the first sensation of sexual passion. The feeling is there and though she will eventually surrender to it, it frightens her as it should frighten a pure and decorous Victorian girl. But in 1908, James attributes her dread to "the sense of something within herself, deep down, that she supposed to be inspired and trustful passion. It was there like a large sum stored in a bank—which there was a terror in having to begin to spend. If she touched it, it would all come out."

This major change adds much that was not there, even implicitly, in 1881. Dozens of critical essays have quoted the "money in the bank" metaphor to impute corrupt or at least disagreeable qualities to Isabel. That she thinks of her feelings as hoarded money, and of love as disbursement, clearly puts obstacles in the way of reading the character as purely admirable and generous. For our purposes, the phrasing "which she supposed to be inspired and trustful passion" is especially baffling. Does James mean that love founded on misperception is not really love, and that therefore Isabel does not love Osmond? Or that she has mistaken not Osmond but her own feelings toward him, and feels not love but some other, more devious, emotion? The cagey phrasing of the revision has opened the door to many theories, some of great sensitivity and perception, about Isabel's feelings. But her feelings in 1881 present no difficulties and require no theories.

The change of Isabel's sphere from emotional to intellectual has reverberations for other aspects of the book. How can so acute and subtle a mind be so seriously wrong about her surroundings? It is easy to comprehend how the Isabel of 1881 might be taken in. But for Isabel in 1908, as for late James characters in general, only a profound, complete, accomplished conspiracy in the outer world can keep her from seeing what is there. This is the reason why, in the revision, Madame Merle and Osmond lose such good qualities as they possess in the original, and are turned into wholly devious and shallow people. Their modicum of natural warmth and their substantial capacities disappear; both become mere swindlers.

Madame Merle when introduced in chapter 18 is originally said to be playing the piano with the touch of an artist, but she is reduced to a performer with skill and feeling in 1908. As [F. O.] Matthiessen has observed, she plays Beethoven in 1881 and Schubert in 1908, which Matthiessen feels is "more within Madame Merle's compass." But of course her compass is defined partly by what she plays! Her "fine, frank smile" in the first version becomes "a sort of world-wide smile, a thing that overreached frontiers," while her "ardent" impulses become only "strong" and, in a later chapter, her "sagacity" is reduced to "tact." For Matthiessen, these changes make "her character unmistakable to the reader," but their evident result is not to clarify, but to change the 1881 character by eliminating frankness, warmth, and spontaneity.

Her artificial and exploitative nature is stressed at every turn. "A brilliant fugitive from Brooklyn" in 1881, she is called (chap. 19) a "perverted product of their common soil" in 1908. She tells Isabel in 1881 that the English "were the finest people in the world" but in 1908 that they are "the most convenient in the world to live with" (chap. 19). The idea that she is always something of a "foreigner" in the original, i.e., that she has an uncomprehended private side, is changed in the revision to the idea that she is always "something of a public performer, condemned to emerge only in character and in costume" (chap. 31), which means that she has no private side.

The image of a character constructed entirely for effect is even more extensively developed in Osmond. James intensifies parts of the 1881 chapter while excising aspects suggesting naturalness and warmth. Osmond in 1881 is a selfish, spoiled, failed, and snobbish man. Nevertheless, there is sincerity in his nature. Rewriting passages about him, James changes his "luminous and intelligent" eyes which express "softness and keenness" to "conscious, curious eyes . . . at once vague and penetrating, intelligent and hard" (chap. 22). Osmond responds "with feeling" in 1881 but "beautifully" in 1908 (chap. 24). The other characters think much less of him, as indeed they ought, in 1908 than in 1881. Ralph compares him in 1881 to a prince who has abdicated in a fit of "magnanimity," but this word becomes "fastidiousness" in 1908 (chap. 23). Mrs. Touchett, who had originally "liked" him because "she thought him so much of a gentleman," now simply "had from far back found a place on her scant list for this gentleman, though wondering dimly by what art and what process—so negative and wise as they were—he had everywhere effectively imposed himself" (chap. 26).

The most substantial change James makes in this character involves a two-page cut—the largest single excision by far in the revision. He takes out a lengthy analysis of Osmond and his motives in chapter 29, but not (as Matthiessen has it) because it is "otiose." The cut considerably changes his interpretation of the character. In the original, Osmond is explained as a selfish man who wanted more than anything in life to succeed. When he falls in love with Isabel, he determines that her admiration will be success enough: "Osmond's line would be to impress himself not largely but deeply; a distinction of the most private sort. A single character might offer the whole measure of it; the clear and sensitive nature of a generous girl would make space for the record." It is true that Osmond sees Isabel only as an admiring audience for his performance, but it is also true that he is content to perform for her alone and that he recognizes her intrinsic qualities.

As he closes up that gap made by the cut, James begins by changing "the desire to succeed greatly—in something or other" to "the desire to have something or other to show for his 'parts' " and concludes by substituting, for Osmond's idea of Isabel as his audience, a more exploitative idea of her as a kind of publicity agent. "His 'style' was what the girl had discovered with a little help; and now, beside herself enjoying it, she should publish it to the world without his having any of the trouble. She would do the thing *for* him, and he would not have waited in vain." He thinks of Isabel only in terms of what she can do for him. She is without intrinsic value, no longer "bright and soft as an April cloud" but "smooth to his general need of her as handled ivory to the palm."

Even though Isabel is a simple character in 1881, the fact that Madame Merle and Osmond are better people means that in an important way she is less taken in by them than is the revised character. Some of the good things that the early Isabel perceives in them are really there. But the finer intelligence of 1908 demands a finer trap, and Merle and Osmond must put on a better show. This requires that they become more complete performers. Because the revisions to this effect deprive them of substance and transform them into empty shells, the heroine of 1908, even though she is so subtle, is paradoxically much more superficial and dense than the Isabel of 1881. She is certainly a worse judge of people, and since she is alone in 1908 in her uncritical evaluation of this pair, she is more stiff and self-righteous in her mistake. This peculiar combination has not struck all readers as attractive, and has given many students of the revised novel a good deal of trouble. This trouble exists to a much smaller degree, if at all, in the early version.

Besides making Osmond and Madame Merle more vicious, James touches almost all of the other characters to reduce them as independent centers of value and judgment. It is as though the younger James had cared for all his characters and tried to give them an illusion of life and depth, while in 1908 only Isabel was real to him. The one character who is not played down is Ralph, in whom James brings out the victimized but transcendent consciousness more than in 1881. Ralph's affinity with Isabel is more pronounced in 1908 than his curiosity or affection. In 1881, his intervention in her life is largely a substitute for an undeclarable love, while in 1908 Isabel is more like an alter ego. He cannot realize his dreams, but possibly she will do it for him. The great moment of the 1908 novel is his death scene—much sentimentalized in the rewriting—when for an instant he and Isabel look at the truth together. This is the union of two consciousnesses. The development of Ralph in 1908 heightens the consciousness theme, and since Ralph's view of Isabel is so uncritical, it also supports the adulatory approach to her character.

The other personalities, however, are flattened and made less genial. Lily (Isabel's sister), Mrs. Touchett, Countess Gemini, and Henrietta—all the other women in the book, in sum—are treated more harshly. An example concerning Lily is worth some examination because it shows the details of James's method. In 1881 (chap. 31), the sisters "had come to Paris, a city beloved by Lily, but less appreciated by Isabel, who in those days was constantly thinking of Rome." In 1908, they "reached the French capital, which was worshipped, and with costly ceremonies, by Lily, but thought of as noisily vacant by Isabel, who in these days made use of her memory of Rome as she might have done, in a hot and crowded room, of a phial of something pungent hidden in her handkerchief." This revision exalts Isabel at the expense of Lily and Paris. The original sentence is mainly informational. It judges neither Paris nor Lily, and by telling us that Isabel was unable to forget Rome lets us know that she is in love with Osmond. The new version makes Paris vulgar and Lily's feelings materialistic, while Isabel's preference for Rome is a sign of aesthetic discrimination. In 1881 she cannot help remembering Rome, but in 1908, on the contrary, memories of Rome are consciously resorted to.

The changes in Countess Gemini alter her nature thoroughly; many of James's revisions seem quite cruel. Presenting her in chapter 24, James changes her "very human and feminine expression . . . by no means disagreeable" to one which, "thanks to various intensities of emphasis and wonder, of horror and joy, was not inhuman." In 1881, she "presented no appearance of wickedness" but in 1908 she "revealed no depths." Her "greeting" to Isabel, than which nothing could have been "kinder or more innocent" in 1881, becomes her "demonstrations" which suggested "the violent waving of some flag of general truce" in 1908. The grotesque exaggerations destroy the character's humanity. When she finally tells Isabel about Merle and Osmond, it is not inappropriate for Isabel, who surmises in 1881 only that the Countess is going to say something "important," to think in 1908 that for the first time she is going to say something "really human." It is difficult to be sure why James discredited the character, but in doing so he certainly nullifies the weight of any of her judgments and opinions. Most particularly, he thoroughly undercuts the many bitter statements she makes about the married woman's lot, statements which have thematic import in the original *Portrait*.

The most important set of changes of this kind result in the systematic vulgarization of Henrietta Stackpole in the 1908 version. Her friend, Bantling, a comic character from the first, becomes sillier in 1908, a change less important in itself than for the way it reflects on her. He is her companion, after all, and to the extent that he is more vulgar, so is she. The relationship is crudely treated: "frank allies" in 1881, they are "groping celibates" in 1908 (chap. 20). Dozens of revisions make Henrietta harsher, more unpleasant, and more stupid. This is important, because Isabel thinks of her in both versions as an "example of useful activity" and takes her for "a model" (chap. 6). In 1881 Isabel is partly measured by her inability to emulate her model; but in 1908 the character is so belittled that the idea of Henrietta as a model is simply absurd. For one thing, James adopts a newly patronizing tone toward her journalistic talents and writings, satirizing aspects of the character which were more respectfully treated in 1881. Though very much a "journalist" and hence not very profound in 1881, she is nevertheless highly talented and thoroughly professional. Quite possible in later years James became more conservative on such issues as woman's equality, but more likely his growing absorption with the inner life made a character who was engrossed in the world of work and action appear inconsequential.

In chapter 10, her first appearance, Henrietta is no longer "decidedly pretty" but only "delicately . . . fair." James removes the approving phrases "very well dressed" and "scrupulously, fastidiously neat," substituting for the latter phrase "crisp and new and comprehensive as a first issue before the folding." In 1881 she "carried not an ink-stain" while in 1908 she "had probably no misprint." The point of the 1881 description is to demonstrate that Henrietta is not a stereotyped female journalist, unsexed and unkempt. She is pretty, decorous, and ladylike. The later images stress her modernity and brashness, turning her into a different cliché—the tough, efficient career girl. Removing the element of softness and personal understatement from Henrietta's character, James makes her loud, overbearing, and obnoxious.

The process extends to very fine details. And 1881 image of her eyes as large polished buttons (chap. 10) expands in 1908 to "buttons that might have fixed the elastic loops of some tense receptacle,' introducing tension into a previously serene character. The originally "brave" Henrietta "went into cages" and "flourished lashes, like a spangled lion-tamer" in revision. The spangles are out of keeping with her earlier sartorial decorum, and the flourished lashes bring a new image of aggressiveness to the depiction. When he changes "Miss Stackpole's brilliant eyes expanded still further" to "ocular surfaces" which "unwinkingly caught the sun," he is certainly making her more machine-like, and when Ralph's comment that she is "decidedly fragrant" is altered to "Henrietta, however, does smell of the Future—it almost knocks one down!" an image of subtlety is replaced by its opposite. Matthiessen notes some of these changes approvingly, pointing out how James has "brightened every inch" of his portrait; but it is precisely the brightening operation that cheapens the character.

It is odd to read in James's preface to the New York edition the author's apology for Henrietta—as exemplifying "in her superabundance not an element of my plan, but only an excess of my zeal . . . . Henrietta must have been at that time a part of my wonderful notion of the lively"—when one is aware that much of the liveliness was in fact put into the treatment by the revisions. When Henrietta comes to Rome after Isabel has married, we read originally that "her eye had lost none of its serenity" but in the revision that "her remarkably open eyes, lighted like great glazed railway-stations, had put up no shutters" (chap. 47). And the final sentences of the book, which have her "shining" at Caspar Goodwood with "cheap comfort," were also added in 1908.

These revisions are thematically crucial; as I have suggested, Henrietta is originally presented as a partial touchstone for Isabel. In 1881 the two women are more like one another than in 1908, and their stories are both germane to the issue of women's independence. As some critics have observed with surprise, Henrietta is the one character in the novel to achieve a successful and meaningful life. Moreover, she advances many of the most perceptive comments about Isabel, which are constantly being utilized by critics even as they belittle the speaker of them. Henrietta exemplifies a realized independence; she suggests what the "new woman" has and what she lacks, what she gains and what she sacrifices. Finally, she shows clearly by contrast that Isabel is not a new woman despite the goals she sets for herself. The contrast between Henrietta's sense and Isabel's sensibility recalls Jane Austen, and although Henrietta never has importance in the novel comparable to Isabel's, their stories are balanced to a certain extent. She is not merely a *ficelle* in 1881, but has independent function.

It is hardly surprising that twenty-seven busy years after he wrote *The Portrait* James would be unable to reproduce the context from which the work had originally been created. One never steps twice into the same river, and no changing artist can write the same work twice. We can re-capture the context of *The Portrait of a Lady* in 1881 to some extent ourselves by so simply a historical exercise as reading the serialization in the *Atlantic Monthly* from November 1880 through December 1881, amidst many fic-tional and essayistic treatments of the new American girl. "What is this curious product of today, the American girl or woman?" began Kate Gannet Wells in an essay entitled "The Transitional American Woman," which appeared in December 1881 along with the second installment of *The Por-trait*. "Does the heroine of any American novel fitly stand as a type of what she is? And, furthermore, is it possible for any novel, within the next fifty years, truly to depict her as a finality, when she is still emerging from new conditions in a comparatively old civilization, when she does not yet un-derstand herself, and when her actions are often the awkward results of motives, complex in their character, unconsciously [sic] to herself?"

To this contemporary question James's story at once seems to offer a response. A certain fictional formula, too, had already developed for the new American girl; indeed it seems to have developed simultaneously with the obvious and widespread change in feminine aspirations epitomized by (though by no means confined to) the woman's movement. The formula was both a conservative answer to, and a literary exploitation of, the new woman's situation—a modern version of the essential feminine fable, the rescue story. An intelligent and attractive young girl, who is independent and wishes to remain so, is "rescued" from this false conception of an appropriate feminine life, by love and marriage. When she falls in love, the natural impulses denied by her desire for independence assert themselves. She finds independence incompatible with a woman's way of living. But this is a happy discovery, for the traditional feminine life fulfills her, and she learns the error of her earlier aspirations. An interesting example of the formula appeared concurrently with *The Portrait* in the *Atlantic Monthly* from June through November of 1881. This was William D. Howell's brief novel, *Dr. Breen's Practice.* In this rather weak story, the heroine is a young doctor who gives up her career after her first patient because she becomes conscious of her psychological unfitness for professional pressure and responsibility. As the wife of a mill owner she will use her traditional medical training in an acceptable feminine way by tending the children of the workers.

This "marriage versus independence" formula is now the most common plot in stories about women. James's use of it can be traced from *Washington Square,* a beautiful and bitter little work which immediately preceded *The Portrait* in composition (and has much in common with it), on to *The Bostonians* in 1886 and *The Tragic Muse* in 1890. It can be associated only with his early phase, when his fiction often dealt with current social material. That the original *Portrait* is controlled by the dynamics of the formal can be seen in the first few chapters, which introduce Isabel amidst conversation about Lord Warburton's need to marry an interesting woman and define her mainly by her fondness for her independence. A reader following the story for the first time would certainly expect Isabel eventually to be brought back into her proper sphere by happy love and see the plot propelled by the question of which suitor could succeed in effecting her rescue. But, as she resists the offers of lovers who believe that they are giving her great opportunities, the embattled Isabel becomes increasingly sympathetic, and when she is finally "saved" from her independence, the event is no rescue but a capture. That is, James uses the popular formula while rejecting its assumptions, so that his form and theme reach beyond formulaic simplification.

Since both Warburton and Goodwood are highly eligible as husbands, the reader may feel that Isabel's solution would have been a different marriage rather than none at all. Critics have mostly believed that Isabel ought to have married and take her severely to task for failing to fall in love with one or the other, dividing into camps according to whom they favor. But the formula proposes love as invariably saving by making young women invariably love wisely, and this is one falsehood James is exposing. Moreover, to assume that Isabel ought to marry because she is female is to beg one of the major questions raised by her story—and, indeed, by the stories of all the other women in *The Portrait,* Henrietta excepted. Many of the critics have just the attitude that disturbs Isabel in her suitors: the presumption that because an offer has been made, she is obligated to accept it or to have an excellent reason for turning it down. Neither Warburton nor Goodwood can accept the idea that she refuses them because she is unwilling to accept any mode of existence that is not self-expressive. But this is Isabel's good transcendental reason (as Quentin Anderson and others have stressed)—this and the unimpeachable emotional truth that she doesn't love either of them.

Warburton "had conceived the design of drawing her into the system in which he lived and moved. A certain instinct, not imperious, but persuasive, told her to resist—it murmured to her that virtually she had a system and an orbit of her own" (chap. 12). It does not matter that the forms of Goodwood's and Warburton's lives are good, and that a woman might live happily and usefully within them. They require the woman to be a satellite in someone else's solar system, and Isabel claims the right to be her own sun. If we define her by membership in the human race rather than the female sex, her claim is admirable. This is how James regards her. He shows it clearly by the fact that Isabel's rejection of Lord Warburton leads Ralph directly to his decision to give her money. The rejection convinces Ralph that her wish for independence is serious and that she is worthy of achieving it. Her wish is thus treated with great respect, not in the least as an aberration.

Ralph is also convinced—wrongly, as it turns out—that a woman could not be strong enough to refuse Lord Warburton unless she had an alternate vision of an independent life. But here Isabel's femaleness does play an important part—brought up female, she has no idea what she might "do" to be independent. The word does not translate into action. This is a terrible limitation, and although James traces its awful consequences, he does not blame her for it. The actual condition of feminine independence, rare as it is, comes about (as Henrietta's story demonstrates) less by choice than necessity, is expressed in unremitting commitment and hard work, and requires fortitude and ability in unusual degree. For these tough requirements Isabel is unfitted by her protected and insulated background, by her lack of training and discipline, and by a "romantic" temperament encouraged by her circumstances.

Here is a subtlety in James's consideration of the theme: modern as it seems, the desire for independence in a young woman may well represent an old-fashioned feminine ignorance of the real world. Consequently, Ralph's gift is no boon to Isabel, and the covert bequest deprives her of one option she has hitherto successfully employed in threatening situations: the choice of turning it down. The fortune imposes on her a necessity to act for which she is hopelessly unprepared. It is no wonder that her first reactions are depression and restlessness and that, startled into premature action, she becomes conventional and traditional.

Basically, she wants to get rid of the fortune and escape the burdens it imposes on her. Because of this special need she is vulnerable to Osmond in a way that she would not have been were she poor (quite apart from the fact that, then, he would not have been interested in her). Older and wiser than she, he will know how to use the money. His apparent lifelong resistance to commitment corresponds to a negative idea of freedom which now, under the pressure of Isabel's need, transforms itself into a positive goal. Because Osmond is less obviously a product of environment than Goodwood and Warburton, Isabel thinks him more free. More important, no clear shape defines itself for the existence of Osmond's putative wife, and therefore Isabel imagines that as Mrs. Osmond she can shape her own life. Although running from independence by reverting to the traditional pattern of love and marriage, Isabel does so in a way that permits her the illusion that she is still seeking freedom. Thus, though the cage she runs into is much smaller than she anticipated, there is no denying that her first free action was to put herself into it. James's point is not that the desire to be independent is dangerous in itself, but that such a desire when its substance is all romantic is no different from any other romantic dream, and will meet the same defeat in real life.

Yet surely he could have established this point without making Osmond and Merle so treacherous. The melodrama of Isabel's later situation certainly detracts from the novel's social realism, and makes her story more specialized, less universal, than it appeared at first. But there is a reason for the many ugly interactions and dreadful revelations of the last third of the book. They push Isabel to the inevitable point of leaving Osmond. This eventuality is much on her mind. As a conventional woman with no more idea than before of how she might live independently, Isabel shrinks from the possibility but cannot see how it can finally be avoided. "She seemed to see, however, the rapid approach of the day when she would have to take back something that she had solemnly given. Such a ceremony would be odious and monstrous; she tried to shut her eyes to it meanwhile" (chap. 45). The later events in the book force her to defy Osmond, and she increasingly realizes the groundlessness of all the reasons she can advance to stay with him. The conspiracy against her is necessary for the plot line because her learning of it destroys her last illusion—that she had married Osmond with her eyes open. Since Isabel did not freely choose him but was manipulated into the marriage, she is absolved from the moral obligation to suffer the results of her own decision. Therefore, if she remains with Osmond, it will be for the same kinds of reasons that originally drew her to him—his promise of an escape from independence and its implications.

Thus the question of whether Isabel will leave Osmond, which propels the story in the last third of the novel, continues the theme of female independence beyond Isabel's marriage. Because James has not followed the popular formula into its apotheosis of love and marriage, he is logically pushed to consider the aftermath of a bad union. Though not part of the formula—which did not and is only now beginning to accept divorce as a part of the texture of human social life—the issue of divorce was from the beginning implicated in questions of female independence and had been debated as a separate question since at least the late 1830s. Henry James, Sr., had taken part in an exchange of letters about it in the *Tribune* and declared himself in favor of "freely legitimating divorce, within the limits of a complete guarantee to society against the support of offspring." Thus it is by no means true that only vulgar or profligate people were associated with the cause of liberalizing the divorce laws.

The senior James's remark also explains why Isabel, having been given a child, was made to lose it. As Goodwood says, in his passionate exhortation, "What have you to care about? You have no children; that perhaps would be an obstacle. As it is, you have nothing to consider" (chap. 55). So even this matter is plotted to give Isabel free rein to leave Osmond. And if Isabel cannot bring herself to the modern American solution of divorce— it is so advanced by Henrietta—she can certainly simply separate from Osmond. Obviously, separation carries no social stricture in the world of the novel. Mrs. Touchett is an apostle of propriety, but lives apart from her husband for no reason except that she prefers to. In fact James is not writing about the abstract right or wrong of divorce, and this judgment does not control his plotting. He is considering what a certain kind of character would do in given circumstances. He concludes that Isabel would come very close to breaking with Osmond, but would recoil at the last.

The agent of recoil is Caspar Goodwood, but we must remember that Isabel's alternatives are not all subsumed in the choice between him and Osmond. She has still the alternative of going her own way, but in fact is less able than before to translate this idea into action. If, as a "free" woman, her greatest independent gesture had been to walk alone from Euston Station to her hotel (chap. 31), she realizes when she returns to London that even this motion is beyond her now. "She remembered how she walked away from Euston, in the winter dusk, in the crowded streets, five years before. She could not have done that to-day, and the incident came before her as the deed of another person" (chap. 53).

In contrast, James gives us Henrietta, crossing continents and oceans without flutter. In Henrietta, too, we have evidence that James does not want to say that independence is metaphysically incompatible with love and marriage. Despite the rather cynical portrayal of love and marriage in most of his fiction, he does not go so far as this in *The Portrait*. The independent spirits in the book—Henrietta and Bantling—fall in love and plan to marry, and this is presented as a happy event. Isabel's disappointment in her friend for showing such weakness is only an extension of her own disillusionment. James's idea, however, seems almost to be that the real possibilities of love and marriage are to be experienced only by those who do not depend on them to give life meaning.

James sympathizes with Isabel's ideals, deplores the external obstacles that thwart them, and still objectively shows how much the obstacles are internal, in Isabel's inadequate preparation for and understanding of the life she thinks she has chosen. He also appears to suggest that those whose romantic idealism may most attract them to this "modern" goal may be the least fitted to achieve it because romantic idealism is other-worldly. His own attraction to the romantic idealist as a type enabled him to bind all this into a single structure with an appropriate tone.

The text of 1908 is not sufficiently revised to transform the work into a late James piece, but is enough changed to cloud the original dynamics of the story. It is a baffling and problematical work, much more so than the text of 1881. The changes created many of the problems. They override the social theme of the work and partly erase it. The matrix of values which radiates out from "independence" in 1881 centers in "awareness" in 1908, with attendant dislocations of emphasis. Awareness in 1881 is a means toward the end of an independent life; in 1908 the independent life is attained only in awareness—the two things are almost identical. The only possible independence is the independence of perfect enlightenment. Consequently, Isabel is no longer perceived as having failed, and, not having failed, she has no limitations or shortcomings of thematic consequence.

Objects of Value: Isabel and Her Inheritance

Elizabeth Allen

With the death of Mr Touchett and Isabel's inheritance, enough money "to meet the requirements of . . . [her] imagination," [*The Portrait of a Lady*] changes. Hitherto, in keeping with Isabel's own self, it has been largely theoretical. Isabel has been seen in conjunction with a gallery of different people, a lot of theoretical discussions have taken place. Now, while Isabel still ponders on the possibilities opening up to her, practical schemes are erected around her.

Isabel becomes aware of the pressure of the potential that her inheritance carries with it. She feels "that to be rich was a virtue because it was to be able to *do*." The need to go beyond the acceptance of the passive female identity is accentuated by the new horizons opening up. Money, she concludes:

> was the graceful contrary of the stupid side of weakness—especially the feminine variety. To be weak was, for a delicate young person, rather graceful, but, after all, as Isabel said to herself, there was a larger grace than that.

Money is a source of power and a potential for action, it makes tangible the spiritual potential that Isabel has signified. Given the economic base to her ideals, Isabel is finally brought face to face with the irresistible need to do something, and the nature of the available choices, and the extent to which her imagination is limited and defined by them, is fully exposed,

From *A Woman's Place in the Novels of Henry James.* © 1984 by Elizabeth Allen. Macmillan, 1984.

Isabel cannot imagine a course of action which has no existence, in, or relation to, a society where women live through and for their husbands, fathers and sons.

Crossing the channel to Italy suggests the continuation of the journey into the world that Isabel began when she ventured out of her room in Albany. The first two chapters set in Italy act in direct contrast to one another, a contrast that is central to the direction of Isabel's journey. In the first, Ralph and Isabel have a friendly discussion about how Isabel can now act, about the need for her to "live" and to be strong. It all sounds very convincing. In the second, we pan in on a picture as deliberately composed and as laden with implication as our opening picture of tea on the lawn at Gardencourt. Osmond's villa has windows which "seemed less to offer communication with the world than to defy the world to look in."

Yet we do look in, on a room full of beautiful objects of which Osmond's daughter Pansy is the most valuable and significant. Madame Merle and Osmond's discussion of Pansy is an overt acknowledgement of the manipulation of the feminine that they practice on Isabel in a more sophisticated form. In the smooth-running machinery of the world as it is, the female is acted upon, like Pansy, or serves the male by acting upon, by offering up its sisters and daughters in the way that Madame Merle serves Osmond. Pansy is "a passive spectator of the operation of her fate" and "impregnated with idea of submission." She is the arch-feminine, child in the adult world. As the betrayal of Isabel takes its course, this female principle, embodied in Pansy, it to become the bone of contention between Osmond, Madame Merle—the woman who sacrifices the principle to the man—and Isabel, who struggles to invest it with some dignity and autonomy. However, at this stage, Pansy is not contended over, but calmly allotted to everyone's satisfaction.

Madame Merle and Osmond then discuss Isabel's attributes, especially her fortune. While she and Ralph are building spiritual castles, her money and her beauty are being weighed up against Osmond's capacity for boredom.

Isabel recognises the contrivance of everything that surrounds Osmond; "even Mr Osmond's diminutive daughter had a kind of finish that was not entirely artless." Yet she cannot place the man himself in any one category: "Her mind contained no class offering a natural place to Mr Osmond—he was a specimen apart." This seems to be part of his appeal for Isabel, he has the charm of the mysterious and also he does not suggest any system or scheme of demands that would engulf her. The aesthetic basis of collecting and admiring is one which maintains a distance, which suggests a certain untouchable quality. Earlier we have been told that there is something "pure and proud" that holds her back from intimacy; but the intimacy of a totally defined and static relationship and one which Isabel feels she is helping to create through her money, is a more acceptable proposition—at least she will not have to become part of a preexisting system, but can make her own. The unwillingness to commit herself is balanced by the desire to do something that she has controlled by the deliberation of her assent to it. Thus when Osmond proposes "she answered with an intensity that expressed the dread of having, in this case too, to choose and decide." Yet when Osmond then stresses her importance to him "Isabel looked at herself in this character—looked intently, thinking she filled it with a certain grace." Isabel is struck with Pansy's helplessness, her dependence on the benevolence of those around her and her lack of will to act on her own behalf: "She would have no will, no power to resist, no sense of her own importance."

Unable to perceive that she has been seen and placed in the same kind of way as she sees Pansy, Isabel assumes that she is making a free choice. As marriage and the assumption of a life in relation to a man seems to be the only mode of action, she attempts to control it by defining her position within her action. There is stress at this point on Isabel's seriousness, her literal reading of the world, which inevitably causes a degree of moral blindness. Osmond calls to this side of her, and the narrowness that lack of humour can cause is later revealed to her, in a horrifying recognition of how "He took himself so seriously; it was something appalling."

It is made quite plain how Osmond objectifies Isabel, how he is prepared to subordinate her to his requirements. Thus he judges her as to whether she will enhance his status and position. He likes her having rejected Lord Warburton, "he perceived a new attraction in the idea of taking to himself a young lady who had qualified herself to figure in his collection of choice objects by declining so noble a hand." And he prepares now to refine her very imagination as a process of amusing himself; her intelligence "was to be a silver plate . . . that he might heap up with ripe fruits, to which it would give a decorative value, so that talk might become for him a sort of served dessert." And he is prepared to "tap her imagination with his knuckle and make it ring." He talks to Isabel about the attempt to make life into a work of art. She takes this as a process which they will create together. He takes her as a part of his pattern, she is to be certain things and not others, and he is quite prepared to sacrifice those of her ideas that he doesn't like. It is Osmond's apparent disregard for society that encourages Isabel to feel she will be free from externally imposed values—she thinks that her active step has been the perception of Osmond's fineness, despite all social disapproval. As Caspar Goodwood shrewdly says to her: "And you don't mean in the least that he's a perfect nonentity. You think he's grand, you think he's great, though no-one else thinks so." And Isabel's response to Ralph's truth-telling is also revealing: "You're going to be put in a cage." "If I like my cage that needn't trouble you." By building her own picture frame, she feels she retains control over the picture, over how she is for herself and the world, but she builds it with far too little understanding of what will make up the cage, and how it will confine her.

Just before the marriage, the final warning is sounded, we are shown Pansy again, Pansy whose "good manners are paramount." She behaves so perfectly that one can only wonder "what penalties for non-performance she dreaded!"

There is a time lapse, and we return to the marriage already a few years old. From this point onward, the situation of Pansy is in the foreground. She becomes the point over which Isabel and Osmond confront each other. The world of abstract theories and choices has hardened into a specific relationship of owner and owned, subject and object. The power accruing to the owner, the wealthy, the man in control of resources can render the less powerful culturally other or momentarily feminine. Thus Ned Rosier, though generally existing as a man and thus as subject in relation to women, can be rendered object in relation to Osmond. He regards Pansy as a—beloved—object: "He thought of her in amorous meditation a good deal as he might have thought of a Dresden-china shepherdess." When he approaches Osmond, he puts himself in the "Pansy" position, saying "I'm afraid that for Mr Osmond I'm not—well, a real collector's piece."

The process of looking is specifically linked now to that of assessment and manipulation, when Rosier goes to Roccanera to see Osmond "he had never in his life felt himself so efficiently looked at."

Isabel looked without judging, either in the worldly sense or in the moral—which would have needed an awareness of the worldly. Now her own glances have been stilled, she no longer signifies potential, she has assumed a static, masklike quality. Her first appearance after her marriage is counterpointed to her initial one in Gardencourt. Now, as then, she is in black:

> The years had touched her only to enrich her; the flower of her youth had not faded, it only hung more quietly on its stem. She had lost something of that quick eagerness to which her husband

had privately taken exception—she had more the air of being
able to wait. Now, at all events, framed in the gilded doorway,
she struck our young man as the picture of a gracious lady.

Isabel is at once more opaque and more public. We look at her for some
time before we are shown her feelings again. As for us, so it is now for
Ralph; for whom Isabel is now inscrutable:

if she wore a mask it completely covered her face. There was
something fixed and mechanical in the serenity painted on it;
this was not an expression, Ralph said—it was a representation,
it was even an advertisement.

As a specific representation or sign, Isabel is now part of a system of
understood communication and action; whereas before she suggested possibilities, she now suggests a static aesthetic and social value. The potential
for a reciprocal action, for her effecting change as well as being looked at
as a "given," for her existing for her own vision as well as for others, has,
for the time, been lost. She is more public, just as Madame Merle (at one
end of the scale) and Pansy (at the other) are public.

Because Isabel appears so different to Ralph and her other friends, and
because it is not merely a quantitative but a qualitative difference—she is
an opaque representation—we see the constructed nature of her existence
now, and the aspects of herself that it represses:

The novel is not merely the conservative response to womanhood, nor the realization of a gracious lady, but a realization of
her picture. What we see in the frame alerts us to the excluded
space outside it. The adorable object is not "nature," but a specific product within a specific system. (J. Goode, "Woman and
the Literary Text." *The Rights and Wrongs of Women*, ed. J. Mitch-
ell and A. Oakley. Penguin, 1976.)

It is the presentation of Isabel within the picture frame, in contrast to her
presented previous hopes and present suffering, which provokes questions.
Pansy, for instance, is presented as the passive, well-behaved little girl. Our
sense of her restriction as image, as "a specific product within a specific
system" comes from Isabel's response to her as the feminine principle which
was appropriated in herself. In growing consciousness of her self as object
for the world, in Osmond, Isabel has to build up her subject identity in
acceptance and recognition of the portrait, the gracious wife that she has
become. Yet this kind of conscious alienation cannot protect her from

increasing perception and increasing unhappiness in response to her conflicting existence as self and other. Repression of this probing unhappiness
results in passivity, which, in turn, exacerbates her position as feminine
and powerless. Isabel attempts merely to be what she appears, imitating
Madame Merle's "firm and bright" qualities. Yet she is aware of the limits
of such patient repression; faced with Lord Warburton, who has given
himself a new sense of purpose with his involvement in politics, she "gave
an envious thought to the happier lot of men, who are always free to plunge
into the healing waters of action." Action is precisely what Isabel thought
herself capable of. Now, it appears, she knows better. Yet she instinctively
recognises that passivity and repression of self precipitates suffering, once
it is self-conscious. She simply cannot envisage a mode of action now, but
she "could never rid herself of the sense that unhappiness was a state of
disease—of suffering as opposed to doing. To 'do'—it hardly mattered
what—would therefore be an escape."

Isabel has not just stayed beautiful, she has lost her sense of flux, of
potential. Ralph muses that "The free, keen girl had become quite another
person; what he saw was the fine lady who was supposed to represent
something." The only action and change open to Isabel now is that of
comprehension of the processes of signification, and her place within them.
Through understanding her manipulation as sign, she will be equipped to
build up some sense of herself in relation to the world, and perhaps some
idea of how to control her function in that relation. But as yet Isabel cannot
open herself to understanding how completely she has been objectified, her
sense of identity still needs some illusion of subjective control. So she views
her situation as self-determined, as a failure of judgement, she cannot yet
see the way she has been manipulated. That would involve a recognition
of the real extent of social imposition, going far beyond the need for correct
clothing. Even on seeing Madame Merle and Osmond together, on catching
a glimpse of their relation to one another, she represses its implications.
Her sense is mainly one of suffocation and darkness "as if Osmond deliberately, almost malignantly, had put the lights out one by one." And her
only energies lie in the resistance to Osmond's and Madame Merle's plans
for Pansy. If Isabel knows that Osmond is not what she thought, she also
realizes that she is not what he expected:

> There were times when she almost pitied him; for if she had not
> deceived him in intention she understood how completely she
> must have done so in fact . . . she had made herself small, pre-
> tending there was less of her than there really was.

Her honesty is internal now, kept for this sort of fireside meditation. In front of others she dissimulates, for various reasons—if she presented only a certain image of herself when Osmond was courting her, it was a deceptive process engendered by him which now extends to her relationship to the whole world. She pretends to them all.

The issue of Pansy's marriage becomes an arena in which Osmond determines to force Isabel to act against her will. She refuses to surrender her integrity, to comply in the conscious and heartless disposal of the submissive and self-denying girl. It is as though Isabel is being asked to admit the lack of self-existence of the young girl she once was, to compound her own guilt in having wanted anything for herself by denying Pansy's right to any honest emotion of her own. Appearances still matter to Isabel, she still feels some retention of control over her existence if she can sustain them, and thus the moral imperative to resist Osmond's plans for Pansy (and his attitude towards her seeking her old friends) involves her in a struggle more painful than that of simply admitting her own conflict with Osmond to him:"To break with Osmond once would be to break for ever; any open acknowledgement of irreconcilable needs would be an admission that their whole attempt had proved a failure." The "whole attempt" includes, after all, Isabel's engagement with the world in an active sense.

Understanding and consciousness, and with them a relaxation of mask and image, finally work through Isabel. She starts to mistrust Madame Merle without knowing why; she feels a "consciousness of respite" when that lady is away from Rome. When Henrietta arrives, she is able to admit to her that she is sad. In Isabel's changed circumstances, the other characters have been thrown into a kind of moral relief by their response to her. The laughable and decadent Countess at least recognises Isabel's worth, and Henrietta would do anything she could to help her. Neither of them see Isabel so much as the situation she is in, their vision is less rigid than that of the world which sees her simply as the gracious portrait. When Caspar comes to see Isabel before leaving Rome and says to her what Ralph had privately thought, that she is "so still, so smooth, so hard. You're completely changed. You conceal everything," she admits to him as well that she is sad, that he may pity her.

When Isabel finally understands just how she has been used, it is as though she seemed "to wake from a long pernicious dream." As she begins to perceive, to see within and beyond the images and appearances, her feeling and understanding become active and living rather than theoretic or repressed. The language is of movement: "It had come over her like a high surging wave." Whereas Madame Merle can say to Osmond "You've not only dried up my tears; you've dried up my soul"; when Isabel finally learns Pansy's true parentage, she can weep for Madame Merle, her first tears for a long time.

Recognising the appropriation incarnate in Osmond, Madame Merle has subordinated herself to it as a woman, and in his interests has sacrificed another woman. By resisting this pattern, Isabel retains her ability to weep, to respond generously. At an internal level, she refuses to become totally a victim of the structure which makes her object, neither is she prepared to try and exploit it. She insists on her consciousness as independent subject.

As Osmond loses his grip on Isabel, he tightens it on Pansy. Pansy's attempts at passive resistance can be easily crushed, not least because she is materially as well as ideologically a helpless person. Not equipped with any of the economic necessities for autonomy that made Isabel's dilemma seem a real one, she can go only where she is put. When we first saw Pansy she was straight from the convent in much she same way as Isabel was straight from her pure, isolated little world in Albany. The repression overtly displayed in sending Pansy back to the convent suggests the kind of repression that Osmond practices in a more sophisticated and less successful form on Isabel—by trying to isolate her from her old friends. Isabel's capacity to resist is strengthened by her growing consciousness of the unacceptable nature of what Osmond does; the only alternative to resistance would be a retreat into passive innocence again. Once awake, whether to understanding or, like poor Pansy, to love, it is meaningless (and Pansy finds almost unbearable) to go back out of the world again. Pansy can gain a reprieve by promising to play according to the rules by denying the self-discovery she has made. Isabel is not prepared to do that, her powers of resistance are stronger, her situation less easy to force. Images continue to break and move, her consciousness is described as a sea. Isabel now sees the connections, the organic nature of things. Her world is no longer controlled by categories which stand fixed and immutable. She made static functions for herself and others, and seeing how the same has been done to her, the language of static image breaks down. Seeing Madame Merle in the convent she notes that "The effect was strange . . . her appearance in the flesh was like suddenly, and rather awfully, seeing a painted picture move." Isabel is now "far afloat on a sea of wonder and pain."

Isabel's innocent interpretations of the world, although engendered by that same world's tendency to interpret reality through the control of signification, never involved a desire to use the people so docketed, more a desire to control how she was seen by ordering what she saw. Now she ˜ees how such designation can render a person secondary to their usefulness as sign, they become simply a thing—and not even an abstract, idealised thing but a minimised reduced object to be utilised. She sees "the dry staring fact that she had been an applied handled hung-up tool, as senseless and convenient as mere shaped wood and iron."

The fear of being used and confined spreads to an awareness of the potential for this not simply, specifically, in Osmond and Madame Merle, but in the way the world works, in the weight of social institution. The convent confining Pansy is an expression of this as much as it is an expression of Osmond's will. Suddenly things connect and interrelate in a way that Isabel has never allowed them to before:

> Now that she was in the secret, now that she knew something which so much concerned her and the eclipse of which had made life resemble an attempt to play whist with an imperfect pack of cards, the truth of things, their mutual relations, their meaning, and for the most part their horror, rose before her with a kind of architectural vastness.

In recognising the relations and structures of events, Isabel recognises the *process* of signification in which the existence of a sign communicated between subjects fixes that sign as secondary, as functioning for another, regardless of the nobility or meanness of what is signified. Isabel's developing consciousness is aided by a period of withdrawal from the world, which takes place in a journey away from Italy and back to England. Here she meditates and confronts what has happened. Yet there is no sense for a moment of any kind of complete withdrawal. Her fear of the "surrender of a personality," that she felt on Pansy's behalf when faced by the convent, is equally strong for herself. Though she recognises the pull of the temptation that Pansy had succumbed to in the end, that of ceasing to resist, and she envies Ralph dying, yet "Deep in her soul . . . was the sense that life would be her business for a long time to come." Painfully Isabel relinquishes both the blankness of surrender and the illusion of total freedom. Everyone is subject to the "mutual relations" of things, even Henrietta, who, in deciding to marry "had confessed herself human and feminine. Henrietta whom she had hitherto regarded as a light, keen flame, a disembodied voice."

Significantly Henrietta now also announces her determination to "grapple in earnest with England." Commitment, even at this comic level, must be both internal and external, personal and social. Freedom means a denial of the feminine, for the feminine is not free, and Henrietta, whatever Osmond thinks, is as inescapably feminine as Isabel.

Returning to Gardencourt, Isabel's sense of human existence is now in direct contrast to its setting and its possessions; her new sense of flux is something she is only beginning to come to terms with. We are told that "She envied the security of valuable 'pieces' which change by no hair's breadth, only grow in value, while their owners lose inch by inch youth, happiness, beauty." The sterility of attempting to experience life as an object in an artistic collection is exposed by implication as self-delusion. Similarly Mrs Touchett, who has been successful in fending off human experience, is now exposed as empty. She has had to deny human relations in order to avoid personal and specific control of herself as sign, so now she will be "an old woman without memories."

As Ralph and Isabel finally acknowledge the truth between them, and abandon all looking at each other for a mutual looking at the truth together, it is Ralph who comes down on the side of the world as having ultimately used Isabel more than she used it or herself. He recognises the extent to which she could never have seen properly in a world which would not admit that kind of independent sight, and says to her "You wanted to look at life for yourself—but you were not allowed; you were punished for your wish. You were ground in the very mill of the conventional!"

Isabel's existence as conscious subject, asserted out of her recognition of her social manipulation as other, gains substance through being communicated externally to Ralph. His death forestalls any possibility of the two presenting any real challenge to existing structures.

As Isabel remains in Gardencourt for Ralph's funeral, the ends running through from her first experiences there are tied up by a sort of reexperiencing of them with much greater clarity. She recognises what is of value, "the beauty of the day, the splendour of nature, the sweetness of the old English churchyard, the bowed heads of good friends." And she finally confronts the last temptation, and the strongest, to surrender the painful burden of consciousness. When Caspar meets her for the last time in the garden the violence of his passion is openly met by a violence of surrender in her. The flux which has been an opening up of her perception has also resulted in a confusion which is precipitated by the sexuality, the abandonment of the social world of appearances, that Caspar represents. As he says, "It's too late to play a part." The imagery is totally physical—of desert winds and white lightning—yet this sense of deluge is internal, confusions are "in her own swimming head." Surrender to the physical world would be a denial of consciousness, of all she has learned concerning the social shell, of the relation of appearances to reality. She knows that submission to Caspar, to passion, would be "the next best thing to her dying," yet also, like dying, it would be a blacking out of the vision she has so lately won. Here the female surrender to sexuality is precisely that—surrender. It involves loss of self, just as being a spiritualised feminine sign does. Just as the nineteenth-century feminists often reacted against ideas of sexual freedom because they saw them as encroaching on their personal and intellectual autonomy by imposing their "sex" on them too strongly, so it is as a part of the same retention of self, of a self-perceived being, that Isabel rejects Caspar. She goes back to Europe, back to the field of experience, resistance and continuing life.

Act of Portrayal

David M. Lubin

In order to demonstrate how Isabel can be viewed as a portrait of a portraitist—in other words, as an instance of self-portraiture by James—it is necessary to identify her characteristic cognitive activities and show how these are the same as those employed by the artist engaged in portrayal. Throughout [*Act of Portrayal: Eakins, Sargent, James*] we have been regarding portrayal as a process that embodies a dialectical interaction. The interaction takes place between the artist's more or less passive observation of what appears as a preexistent reality (the sitter: the portrait's so-called subject) and the artist's more or less active construction of a material artifact (a painting, a novel) that activates and manipulates various cultural codes in order to produce something that the viewer will read similarly to, but also differently from, how he would have read the antecedent reality. To the extent that passive observation is stereotyped by our society as feminine, while instrumental activity is characterized as masculine, the act of portrayal as it is here defined might be regarded as an activity involving dually sexual, antithetically sexual, impulses.

Before turning to *The Portrait of a Lady* itself to see how Isabel "is like" a portraitist, perhaps it would first be best to see how James conceived of literary portraiture, the activity that he performed as he proceeded to write the novel. The 1908 preface to the New York edition of *The Portrait* starts with an account of the material circumstances involved in the production of the earlier text. Specifically, James speaks of Venice, where he

From *Act of Portrayal: Eakins, Sargent, James.* © 1985 by Yale University. Yale University Press, 1985.

wrote the latter portions of the novel, and of the difficulties he had finding his concentration in such an abundantly interesting, hence distracting, locale. He is not, at this opening point in the preface, talking about characterization; that comes later. Yet since the theory of characterization, of portrayal, is the preface's chief concern, perhaps this initial discussion of Venice is at least metaphorically related to it.

"I had rooms on Riva Schiavoni, at the top of a house leading off to San Zaccaria;" he says, then continues:

> The waterside life, the wondrous lagoon spread before me, and the ceaseless human chatter of Venice came in at my windows, to which I seem to myself to have been constantly driven, in the fruitless fidget of composition, as if to see whether, out in the blue channel, the ship of some right suggestion, of some better phrase, of the next happy twist of my subject, the next true touch of my canvas, mightn't come into sight. But I recall vividly enough that the response most elicited, in general, to these restless appeals was the grim admonition that romantic and historic sights offer the artist a questionable aid to concentration when they themselves are not to be the subject of it. They are too rich in their own life and too charged with their own meanings merely to help him with a lame phrase; they draw him away from his small questions to their own greater ones; so that, after a time, he feels, while thus yearning toward them in his difficulty, as if he were asking an army of glorious veterans to help him arrest a peddler who has given him the wrong change.

Just as Venice with its ceaseless human chatter and its wonderous lagoon distracts the novelist from his labor without in return supplying some right suggestion to help steady the fruitless fidget of composition, so, it might be said, does the closely observed personality of an individual subject resist artistic toil when, like Venice in all its watery depth and multichanneled complexity, it is gazed upon by the would-be portraitist as a model from which to work. "How can places that speak *in general* so to the imagination not give it, at the moment, the particular thing it wants?" James inquires. He then replies, "The real truth is . . . that [scenic locales] express, under this appeal, only too much—more than, in the given case, one has use for."

Certainly James could not have continued to look out his window onto the Riva Schiavoni and still have written his novel. He had to turn away from that window; he had to shut out the view; he had to cut down the field of vision; he had to suppress. This, it seems, is what every portraitist must do: he must look away from the immensity and flux, the only too much, and turn instead to text or canvas, where an orderly, manageable, circumscribed version of reality's immensity and flux can be set forth.

For James, the genuine artist views through the open window "the faintest hints of life," and then, presumably when focused again on the uncompleted page or canvas, "converts the very pulses of the air into revelations." Implied in this artistic labor is a shuttling back and forth between the window from where the flux of any external reality such as the individual personality is detected, and the desk or easel where a much reduced version of that reality is put together. Hence the dialectic we spoke of earlier [in *Act of Portrayal*]: the productive conflict between observation and creation, between the relatively passive and relatively active modes, between taking things in (perception) and then, after changing their shape, thrusting them out again into something else (penetration). Much of the tension that animates *The Portrait of a Lady* results from a similar conflict or set of conflicts experienced by the protagonist, Isabel, who, as we shall see, yearns for reality unconstricted, uncropped, and yet at the same time for reality that is delimited, structured, graspable.

We might characterize the twin but antithetical impulses of the portraitist (whether Henry James or Isabel Archer) this way: as realism and formalism. The realist impulse, as used here, is the wish to perceive and record the object of observation, be it oneself, another person, a social formation, or whatever, as completely and with as little intervention as possible by the medium of reproduction. The formalist impulse, however, is one that finds pleasure or value not so much in what is being observed, but rather in the way that it is being observed and the way it is being reproduced. The difference here is between an impulse that favors content prior to its formalization, and another that is less interested in the "prior" content than in the resulting form into which that content is artistically translated.

A good example of a literary realist—using the term as given here—is the sixteenth-century French essayist Michel de Montaigne, who says of himself as self-portraitist:

> Others shape the man; I portray him, and offer to the view one
> in particular, who is ill-shaped enough. . . . Now the lines of
> my portrait are never at fault, although they change and vary.
> Everything goes incessantly up and down . . . both with the

universal motion and with their own. Constancy is nothing but a more sluggish movement. I cannot fix my subject . . . I catch him here, as he is at the moment when I turn my attention to him. I do not portray his being; I portray his passage; not a passage from one age to another . . . but from day to day, from minute to minute. I must suit my story to the hour. . . . It is a record of various and variable occurrences, an account of thoughts that are unsettled and, as chance will have it, at times contradictory, either because I am then another self, or because I approach my subject under different circumstances and with other considerations.

Aside from the narrator of *The Sacred Fount,* no Jamesian character, not even Colonel Capadose, the title character of James's story, "The Liar," is permitted the high degree of inconsistency and moment-to-moment changeability that Montaigne perceives in himself and by extension all others. Unlike James, Montaigne shows no interest in discovering and obeying formal principles of character representation: "Could my mind find a firm footing, I should not be making essays, but coming to conclusions," he remarks somewhat waspishly at the end of the passage cited. In such open-ended works as *The Portrait,* James is certainly far from the simplistic coming to conclusions that Montaigne denigrates, yet nevertheless the very nature of his formalist imperative dictates the superimposition of closure, symmetry, and totality onto the human subject that is being portrayed.

There comes at a later point in the 1908 preface James's often-noted "house of fiction" metaphor. In this metaphor, the enterprise of literature is likened to a huge mansion with many windows, behind each of which stands a figure (a writer) who is peering through a spyglass (an individual sensibility) at the surrounding environment (reality). Since no two windows are positioned alike, no two observing figures will have the same perspective on that environment. In terms of the realist-formalist dichotomy described above, when James the portraitist is at the window of the house of fiction, "a figure with a pair of eyes, or at least with a field glass," he is the openly observing Montaignesque realist unperturbed by the inconsistency, flux, and infinite detail of the individual personalities at which he gazes. When he is at the desk of this house, however, the formalist takes, or at least seeks, command, and in so doing strips these personalities of their immense complexity by translating them into literary concepts, categories, and effects. To some degree this conflict between what is perceived as an outside, prior reality and the subjection of that so-called reality to conventions of aesthetic form underlies virtually every act of artistic creation, not only those of portraiture, and certainly not only those of Henry James (and Thomas Eakins and John Singer Sargent). Indeed, this conflict is latent even in our day-to-day acts of selective perception, wherein we unconsciously fit sensory data to preestablished categories or, if such data will not fit, disregard it altogether: "If we had a keen vision and feeling of all ordinary life, it would be like hearing the grass grow and the squirrel's heart beat, and we should die of the roar which lies on the other side of silence," notes George Eliot, adding, "As it is, the quickest of us walk about well wadded with stupidity."

But even if this conflict is inherent in virtually every artistic creation, there are certain works that particularly strive to bring it to the fore, and that includes, if not every major portrait by James, Eakins, and Sargent, unquestionably the three examined here. Already we have seen the conflict in *The Agnew Clinic,* with Eakins-as-artist seeming to ally himself most uncomfortably with both the masculine surgeon-penetrator and the feminine patient-receiver, and then seen it manifested in *The Boit Children,* with Sargent-as-artist identifying himself with the patriarchal force that encloses feminine sensibility and, at the same time, with that sensibility's resistance to patriarchy's excessively logical, symmetrical structures. Now, by looking closely at *The Portrait of a Lady,* we will see how it too is a text whose continuing life and energy is generated from the realist/formalist, feminine/masculine, reception/penetration conflicts that occur at various levels of story and discourse.

Isabel Archer resents being pinned down, labeled, or otherwise put in a box. She adamantly resists any conclusions that others attempt to construct for her or about her. This is especially evident early in the novel, before she is married, but it is equally true through to the end. And well she might be supersensitive to this attempt by others to narrow her down, for from start to finish almost every other character in the book is preoccupied with getting a fix on her and determining with certitude the answer to what James in the preface refers to as "the primary question"—"Well, what will she *do?*"

In Isabel's first conversation with cousin Ralph, for instance, when he jokingly suggests that his mother, Lydia Touchett, has adopted her, the young woman bridles at the very thought: " 'Adopted me?' The girl stared, and her blush came back to her, together with a momentary look of pain which gave her interlocutor some alarm. . . . 'Oh no; she has not adopted me. I'm not a candidate for adoption. . . . She has been very kind to me;

but,' she added with *a certain visible eagerness of desire to be explicit,* 'I'm very fond of my liberty' " [italics mine].

The reason for my italicizing James's notation about Isabel's visible eagerness is to call attention to this as the first of numerous occasions in the text in which her concern for how she appears to others is brought in to play. Sooner or later the reader begins to see, hidden beneath each of Isabel's assertions of her desire to be free of categories and labels imposed upon her from without, a subtle, evidently unconscious bidding to others to think well of her: to pin her after all, but only as she wishes.

Again, it should be remembered that Isabel's defensiveness is not unjustified: everyone does indeed display, to one degree or another, a proprietary and instrumental interest in her. When Ralph first discusses Isabel with his mother, he asks, "What do you mean to do with her?" (echoing the author's "Well, what will she *do*?"). Soon afterward, Mrs. Touchett aggressively rejects Ralph's assumption that Mr. Touchett will have some say in the young woman's future: "I don't know about that. She's my niece, not his." Ralph's response is "Good Lord, dear mother; what a sense of property!" Yet before long Aunt Lydia has grounds to strike back at her son's way of thinking and of speaking about their relative. "Do with her? You talk as if she were a yard of calico." Indeed, Mrs. Touchett, along with her husband, proves to be one of the only characters in the novel who does not attempt to take literal or epistemological possession of Isabel, or to make use of her for self-interested reasons, monetary, aesthetic, or personal. Warburton, Osmond, Ned, and even Ralph certainly do, as do Henrietta, Pansy, and of course Madame Merle, of whom Isabel says understatedly at the end, "She made a convenience of me." Of the important characters in the novel, only the Touchetts senior and the Countess Gemini can get along perfectly well without her, and therefore have no need to possess her, use her, or imaginatively organize their lives around her.

"Ah, Lord Warburton, how little you know me!" Isabel gently chides when the aristocrat asks for her hand. Nonetheless she is pleased to see that she does "all so mysteriously, matter to him." This two-stage, self-contradicting response typifies Isabel throughout: she resents attempts to pin her down, make sense of her, understand her, always viewing such attempts as misprisions, as false constructions, and yet she hungers to be admired and, in one way or another, desired. This pattern is apparent even in her dismal marriage to Osmond, where her misery stems from being saddled with a husband who not only closes off her possibilities as a free agent, but who also finds in her shamefully little to admire or desire. Perhaps there is expressed here, on Isabel's part, a narcissistic need for self-idealization; she appears to require continuing confirmations from the outside world that her ego-ideal is safe and valid, and at the same time she seems so anxious to avoid denial of this that she fights off any attempts by others to get close to her and know her in depth. My wish in describing Isabel thus is not to indulge in psychologism—the fallacy of treating a verbal, artistic construct, Isabel Archer, as though she were a flesh-and-blood individual who, unlike the fictional character, would undergo psychoanalysis. I do wish, however, to show how her thought and behavior within the narrative of which she is a part are analogous to the mental processes involved in James's act of portraiture (and self-portraiture). In order to accomplish this, it is necessary that we treat Isabel's (and other characters') verbal utterances and narrative behavior as though these were real acts that could be described and analyzed psychologically. Equally important, though, is never to forget that we are sliding back and forth between two desperate ontological categories—human subjects and literary characters.

Warburton to Isabel: " 'You know, if you don't like Lockleigh—if you think it's damp or anything of that sort—you need never go within fifty miles of it. . . . There's no difficulty whatever about that; there are plenty of houses. I thought I'd just mention it; some people don't like a moat, you know. Good-bye.'

'I adore a moat,' said Isabel. 'Good-bye.' "

This banter furthers the text's construction of Isabel as a humanlike character by permitting us to see, through implied meaning and perhaps even by the use of homophony, that what she actually adores is a protective gap between herself and all others, a moat that allows her to remain *remote*.

The desire on Isabel's part not to be fixed or judged, and yet to be thought of in the best light, has perhaps much to do with that remoteness of hers that she sometimes worries makes her "cold, hard, priggish." So long as she is able to maintain her distance from those who attempt closeness, she remains in a protective, defensible position, because those who think well of her will not be permitted an intimacy that might sour their favorable perceptions. Moreover, those who are inclined to make judgments of her have those judgments automatically invalidated, or at least made unverifiable, by that very distance. Transferring for a moment this discussion to the real-world, historical existence of Henry James, we think of his notorious efforts to hide from others, even from so-called intimates, his inner life. Like Isabel in the text, James in the world was interested in deflecting away from himself and onto something else—in this case, his work—the judgments of others and their attempts to be close. He, like Isabel, seems to have adored moats, even if somewhat guiltily, and he made sure that he was always surrounded by one.

The most direct statement of the metaphysic underlying Isabel's defensive remoteness comes in chapter 19, during the debate over the nature of personality that the young woman engages in with Madame Merle. The older woman begins by making a case that in today's terms would be described as behaviorist, inasmuch as she argues that external appearances correspond directly to internal realities, and that the internal reality may accurately be read from external appearances.

> When you've lived as long as I you'll see that every human being has his shell and that you must take the shell into account. By the shell I mean the whole envelope of circumstances. There's no such thing as an isolated man or woman; we're each of us made up of some cluster of appurtenances. What shall we call our "self"? Where does it begin? where does it end? It overflows into everything that belongs to us—and then it flows back again. I know a large part of myself in the clothes I choose to wear. . . . One's self—for other people—is one's expression of one's self; and one's house, one's furniture, one's garments, the books one reads, the company one keeps—these things are all expressive.

Isabel, James tells us, "was unable to accompany her friend into this bold analysis of the human personality." Her view, which is fully in keeping with her desire to be unpinned by social conventions or by people's assessment of her, can be characterized as idealist, a belief which holds that external appearances are not unimpeachable indices to internal realities, and may therefore lead an observer to entirely false conclusions about the nature of those realities. While to Madame Merle's way of thinking, the external and internal so interpenetrate or overflow one another that making distinctions between the two ultimately becomes impossible, Isabel's idealist, essentialist, Emersonian position holds that external and internal are not only distinct, but also inevitably at odds with one another.

> "I don't know whether I succeed in expressing myself, but I know that nothing else expresses me. Nothing that belongs to me is any measure of me; everything's on the contrary a limit, a barrier, and a perfectly arbitrary one. Certainly the clothes which, as you say, I choose to wear, don't express me; and heaven forbid they should! . . . My clothes may express the dressmaker, but they don't express me. To begin with it's not my own choice to wear them; they're imposed upon me by society."

In effect Isabel is saying: "No one has any right to judge me, for I am something entirely separate from the socially and environmentally mediated appearance that you wrongly, very wrongly, scrutinize, quantify, judge, and label as me."

Asserting that we cannot gain accurate knowledge of a person by regarding his appearance, his behavior, or his self-chosen appurtenances as indicators of what lies within, Isabel attacks the very premise underlying all portraiture, written, sculpted, or painted. Her position rests upon an assumption that every human subject has within an inviolable and unquantifiable essence, a soul, that remains unchangingly, uniquely, and entirely apart from whatever transformations time and society may enact upon habits of speaking, behaving, and dressing. This is a Neoplatonic assumption; it involves a conception of reality—*real* reality—as static, fixed, untouched by history, eternally enduring. If Madame Merle claims that a person is nothing more than what one does and how one does it, Isabel thinks instead that one has a residual reality, and that this is the core reality, the true reality, the essence that not only precedes earthly existence but also cannot be reached simply through an empirical, inductive examination of that existence.

Though it would be inaccurate to describe Madame Merle as a dialectical materialist, her position is nevertheless historicist and anti-essentialist: she sees character not as something prior to matter and history, but rather as something that is negotiated anew, moment to moment, by the interactions of both material force and social relations, or, as she puts it, "the whole envelope of circumstances." Thus it would seem that she speaks on behalf of the sort of portraiture James is engaged in, one that attempts to create—to show—character dynamically, developmentally, as an ongoing process rather than as a fixed, static, basically unchanging essence that is only dressed up in the clothes and ideas of time and place for the sake of local color. Earlier I suggested that, to the extent a portraitist allots priority to (material) reality over (abstract) form, he or she is realist rather than formalist. In this sense, then, Merle can be regarded as a spokeswoman for Montaignesque realism in portraiture/character depiction, while Isabel, devaluing material reality and enshrining instead abstract essences, would seem to prefer a portraiture that imposes categorical order on the messy, recalcitrant, inconsistent material reality of human character. This idealist way of thinking causes her to regard those around her as if they were walking and talking manifestations of preexistent forms; hence her frequent reference to other individuals as "types" or "specimens."

Yet neatly to equate Madame Merle's respect for matter with a portraitist's impulse toward realism, and Isabel's preference for intangible abstraction with the contrary impulse toward formalism, would be inadmissibly reductive. Formalism, as described above, can include not only the artist's love for the conventions, categories, and rules of an art, but also the material of it, whether that material is paint or paragraphs. In this regard, then, the artistic formalist can also be a materialist, with the material she or he prefers not so much what is being represented (the human body, let us say) as that stuff (phrases or brushstrokes) employed to build the representation. Therefore, on the formalist side, Merle might be seen representing what can perhaps best be described as material formalism, while those tendencies Isabel stands for can be termed conceptual formalism. The battle lines drawn between Isabel and Merle (first "only" ideological but later, as the plot unfolds, also sexual and proprietary) are lines that position the opposing sides, the clash of which generates James's psychological portraiture. The two major dichotomies are on the one hand between the tendencies of realism, meaning here that the imposition of order never becomes more than a secondary concern, and formalism; and on the other hand, within the formalist camp, between the preconceptual and the promaterial.

To put this another way: the impulses competing with one another in James's literary portraiture are (1) the concern to be true to the human subject or subjects he is depicting; (2) the desire to manipulate not only the tools and the rules of his craft, but also the subject as he has perceived it, in order to achieve a thing of beauty; (3) his intrinsic pleasure in the materials of his trade (words, phrases, rhythmic patterns, and so forth); and (4) his high regard for the moral concepts and humane emotions that can be generated from text to reader by means of the artful arrangement, patterning—in a word, exploitation—of those same materials. Though I am not arguing that *The Portrait of a Lady* is a strictly allegorical display of various impulses battling for supremacy, I am claiming that this conflict at the aesthetic level is ultimately inseparable from the other types of conflict the text embodies.

It will be helpful to look at various characters in the novel vis-à-vis the categories introduced so far, namely, realism, formalism, idealism, and materialism. These categories sometimes blend into one another, so that it would be a mistake to think of any of them as fully isolated from the others; not one of these categories can be conceived alone. Therefore it must be remembered that when we link a certain character with realism and another with idealism, and so on, we are speaking only of general tendencies displayed by this or that particular character in word and deed.

Isabel thinks herself open and adventurous in her attitude toward herself and others. She believes she is ready to cast her gaze unflinchingly and unjudgingly upon the frailties of the human spirit. She is eager, the narrator tells us, to feed her "immense curiosity about life" and to feel "the continuity between the movements of her own soul and the agitations of the world." Following the behest of her recently deceased father, who "had a large way of looking at life," she wishes "to see as much of the world as possible." Yet because she has an imagination that is "remarkably active"—even "ridiculously" active—she possesses the often troublesome "faculty of seeing without judging." Indeed, making final judgments is, she believes, so foreign to her nature that when she was a child during the Civil War, "she felt herself at times (to her extreme confusion) stirred almost indiscriminately by the valour of either army."

It would follow, then, that Isabel's vision of humanity is fully inclusive, fully accepting, the paradigmatic mind set of the neo-Montaignesque realist to whom no behavior is alien. As she says of herself, "I like so many things! If a thing strikes me with a certain intensity I accept it. I don't want to swagger, but I suppose I'm rather versatile. I like people to be totally different from Henrietta. . . . Then Henrietta presents herself, and I'm straightaway convinced by *her*."

Prior to this quotation, however, the narrator had already begun complicating Isabel's view of herself as an all-tolerating, all-encompassing humanist. "Isabel's chief dread in life at this period of her development was that she should appear narrow-minded; what she feared next afterwards was that she should really be so." How she looks to others is clearly different from and more important to her than what she "really" is. Her sense of having a genuine self distinct from external appearances paradoxically puts her in the position of manipulating the image she presents others so that she might save, not so much her integrity, but her own self-image. This is simply one of the ways in which her idealist, essentialist, Neoplatonic beliefs give rise to (or arise from) a constricting mode of perception—for certainly one who dreads appearing or being narrow-minded is not likely to perceive herself or others in a relaxed, tolerant, unrestrictive manner.

Another, and closely related, result (or cause) of her dualistic view of reality is her habit of thinking in types. She sees the people she meets not as unique, idiosyncratic individuals who are an endlessly complex admixture of psychological process and social or economic determination, but rather as flesh-and-blood embodiments of abstract qualities and preestablished categories. This is the conceptual formalism I described earlier, applied however not to aesthetic materials but instead to fellow humans. Isabel makes people fit into slots rather than making her ideological slots fit people.

Her response to Lord Warburton is a good example of this. When Ralph is about to introduce him to her, she exclaims, "Oh, I hoped there would be a lord; it's just like a novel!" A week or so later, she is still regarding him, of course with a touch of irony, as "a hero of romance."

> Isabel had spoken [to Ralph] very often about "specimens", it was a word that played a considerable part in her vocabulary; she had given him to understand that she wished to see English society illustrated by eminent cases.
> "Well now, there's a specimen," he said to her as they walked up from the riverside and he recognized Lord Warburton.
> "A specimen of what?" asked the girl.
> "A specimen of an English gentleman."

Little wonder Warburton chides that she is "always summing people up," and that her mind "looks down on us all," or that he can say, with Henrietta Stackpole in mind, "I never saw a person judge things on such theoretic grounds," only to have Isabel reply, "Now I suppose you're speaking of me."

It is not only Warburton who is the object of this stereotyping method of thinking about people. When Isabel, chatting with her uncle, discussed the neighbors, "she usually inquired whether they corresponded with the descriptions in the books." Such an inquiry as this would bring a "fine dry smile" to the old Yankee pragmatist: " 'The books?' he once said; 'well, I don't know much about the books. You must ask Ralph about that. I've always ascertained for myself—got my information in the natural form. I never asked many questions even; I just kept quiet and took notice.' "

Mr. Touchett, though a minor character, is more than anyone else in the novel an embodiment of that all-tolerating, fully receptive Montaignesque empirical realism that Isabel admires yet does not in any way demonstrate. When Touchett explains that he tries to look at things on their own terms instead of in categories derived from books, he is of course oblivious to the poststructuralist recognition, a century later, that all our day-to-day, common-sense perceptions of reality are unavoidably mediated by our continuous first- and second-hand exposure to "book-learning." Yet nevertheless his quiet, passively receptive approach to looking at the world and people around him is characteristic of the approach to portraiture that James conveyed years afterward by the image of himself looking out his window at "the waterside life, the wonderous lagoon spread before me." As the only genuinely disinterested character in the novel, the only one who is not engaged in an act of seeking (money, experience, freedom, a partner, an edifying or aesthetic spectacle), Touchett is the only character qualified to represent this aspect of portraiture. Otherwise, non-instrumental observation, passive reception, the valuing of things in the natural form, is present in the story only insofar as it is conspicuously absent in the lives of all the other characters.

It is appropriate of Touchett to remark, in the passage above, "You must ask Ralph about that," for like Isabel, Ralph tends to draw categories and remit people to them. "Ralph Touchett was a philosopher. . . . His father, as he had often said to himself, was the more motherly; his mother, on the other hand, was paternal." Ralph considers cousin Isabel, as Selden considers Lily Bart [in Edith Wharton's *The House of Mirth*], a spectacle or entertainment of a high order: " 'A character like that,' he said to himself— 'a real little passionate force to see at play is the finest thing in nature. It's finer than the finest work of art—than a Greek bas-relief, than a great Titan, than a Gothic cathedral. . . . Suddenly I receive a Titan, by the post, to hang on my wall—a Greek bas-relief to stick over my chimney-piece.' " The difference between Isabel and Ralph in this regard is that while she conceives of people in terms of familiar literary characters and types, he thinks of her in terms of lofty aesthetic objects; his manner is perhaps more sophisticated, but equally mediated. How unlike either of the elder Touchetts, both of whom seem to distrust any kind of literary portrayal, whether in a letter, a novel, or a newspaper report. Aunt Lydia, wishing to know about her several nieces, booked passage to America: "There was no need of writing, for she should attach no importance to any account of them she should elicit by letter; she believed, always, in seeing for one's self." Her husband amusedly reminisces about "a lady who wrote novels . . . she was a friend of Ralph's . . . she was not the sort of person you could depend on for evidence. Too free a fancy—I suppose that was it." As concerns journalistic portraiture, Lydia says to Isabel's friend, Henrietta, "We judge from different points of view. . . . I like to be treated as an individual; you like to be treated as a 'party,' the implication being that Henrietta also treats others as parties, or specimens of a type, for the sake of her reports. This is portraiture at its worst that is being mocked, a conceptual formalism exaggerated to the point of mechanical stereotype. Henrietta herself practically admits as much, ironically to be sure, when she speaks to Isabel of her latest transatlantic report: "I was going to bring in your cousin—the alienated American. There's a great demand just now for the alienated American, and your cousin's a beautiful specimen."

Isabel's penchant for fixing the people she knows and pinning them to preestablished categories is illuminated on one side by cousin Ralph's aestheticism and on the other by Henrietta's crassly commercial stereotyping. Taken to the extreme (as perhaps Ralph himself never takes it—unlike Gilbert Osmond), aestheticism, the ardent pursuit of "the sweet-tasting property of the observed thing in itself," leads to making a fetish of the personality under scrutiny, thus dehumanizing that personality, valuing it not in itself (as the Montaignesque realist might do) but for the sake of the sweet-tasting property it permits the scrutinizer to experience. Meanwhile, Henrietta's reduction of every one she meets into a type, a specimen, a party, makes her always abrasive, often comic, and thoroughly successful at her job of manufacturing for her newspaper readers such stock charac-terizations that provide these mass consumers with merely a different, more vulgar variety of sweet-tasting property than that swallowed by the aes-thete. Henrietta's manner of perceiving and representing other people com-modifies them and thus is dehumanizing, but the dehumanization involved is not generically different from that which results from Ralph's aestheti-cism, Osmond's narcissism, and Isabel's idealism. All of these characters—from the heroine to the villain, from the faithful and kind friend to the blustery comedic one—reveal at various levels what, throughout this anal-ysis, we have seen as the chief moral peril of portraiture: rigidification of the subject and its exploitation. Ralph's remark that "there was something in Miss Stackpole's gaze that made him . . . vaguely embarrassed—less inviolate, more dishonoured, than he liked" is merely a subjective statement of what it feels like to be the object of a fixing, penetrating, exploitative gaze, regardless of whether the interest that prompts the gaze is careerist (as with Henrietta), aesthetic (as with Ralph when it is turned upon his cousin), idealistic (Isabel), medical (the students in *The Agnew Clinic*), sexual (Lily Bart's observers in *The House of Mirth*), paternal (the absent father of *The Boit Children*), or artistic (that of the portraitist).

In all of these instances, the subject (the personality being gazed at) is treated as an object (the object of the gaze) and therefore as a whole, a totality, a largely immutable concretion of abstract essences (goodness, wickedness, beauty, and so forth). In their semiological study of ideology, Rosalind Coward and John Ellis observe that the function of ideology is "to fix the individual in place as subject for a certain meaning. This is simultaneously to provide individuals with subject-ivity, and to subject them to the social structure with its existing contradictory relations and powers." According to this argument, the purpose served by treating the subject as a fixed and unified whole is to hide from him (or her) the irre-mediable contradictions upon which both he and his society are predicated. This hiding, this repression, is the work of ideology, and its primary tool is language—an activity that, by its subject-verb format, which confers centrality and will to the I who speaks, teaches every individual in society to regard himself as an unified whole. "Ideologies set in place the individual as though he were this subject: the individual produces himself in this imaginary wholeness, this imaginary reflection of himself as the author of his actions." From this perspective, then, Isabel's idealism, Henrietta's literary consumer commercialism, and Ralph's aesthetic formalism are various enactments of the main business of ideology itself, which is the fixing of the subject, or in other words, the subject's objectification: its being cemented into seemingly noncontradictory, nondialectical, reified object.

The term "subject" makes any discussion such as this especially confusing, because the word has several meanings, all of which are involved. When we are speaking of the subject of a portrait, we might be referring to the individual agent whom the portrait represents, or to the individual who has constructed the portrait, or even to the individual who reads it. To the extent that a portrait presents Subject 1 (the individual portrayed) as a consistent whole, and thus covers over social and epistemological contradiction rather than exposing it, the portrait perpetuates our inbred notion of Subjects 2 and 3 (author and receiver) as both being fixed points of origin, of creativity, understanding, morality, and so forth, which is precisely the traditional teaching of humanism. Humanism, according to Louis Althusser, is that set of beliefs that hopes to "explain society and history, by taking as its starting-point human essence, the free human subject, the subject of needs, of work, the subject of moral and political action." As defined by Althusser, humanism is the benevolent name given to subject-defining, position-fixing, contradiction-reducing ideology. A humanist text does not repress contradiction altogether, for then it would lose its credibility—people do sense, after all, that they embody contradictions, and would not accept as worthwhile anything that completely denies the lived experience—but the humanist text does makes contradiction palatable and readable. It does this by its imposition of aesthetic form.

The humanist text, of which *The Portrait of a Lady* is an example, tolerates a certain amount of contradiction (*The Portrait* highlights, for instance, the contradiction between Isabel's desire to be nonjudgmental and her habitual wedging of people into categories), but presents that contradiction in an orderly, noncontradictory fashion. The balance it achieves between the inconsistency it depicts and the consistency with which it does so conveys to its reader (its final subject, Subject 3) a placating, politically liberal or progressive—and thus never revolutionary—sense that the horrible contradictions of both the individual and his or her society can be either satisfactorily resolved or tolerably accepted. Thus in a humanist text such as this early James psychological portrait, our sense of human indeterminacy is forever moderated and comforted and kept from boiling over into anything approaching radical social action by the implicit message of literary form: order shall prevail. Or, as E. M. Forster maintained, "Novels, even when they are about wicked people, can solace us; they suggest a more comprehensible and thus a more manageable human race, they give us the illusion of perspicacity and power."

Yet even if *The Portrait of a Lady* reinforces and perpetuates the reigning humanist ideology of the fixed, unitary subject by such devices as (a) an implied "I–you" form of address by the narrator, (b) a relatively easy-to-understand prose style that has the effect of making the reader feel he or she occupies a privileged position to look at and understand reality, (c) the "central consciousness" point of view, (d) a heavy reliance on such melodramatic polarities as good/evil, selfish/generous, honest/deceitful, and innocent/corrupt, and (e) the normative regularity with which characters judge and label one another—even so, the text does throw out signals that contradict this dominant thrust. Madame Merle's materialist challenge of Isabel's idealism is an example. True, the reader is eventually made to feel that Merle is evil, and thus is her philosophy condemned by guilt through association, but at least that philosophy, anti-idealist to the core, is enunciated fairly, and at a point in the text before the narrative has turned the reader wholly against its proponent. Similarly, the antiformalist realism of Daniel Touchett is voiced effectively and by a wholly sympathetic character, even though that voice dies with the character early in the story. The fun made of Henrietta Stackpole, who greatly exaggerates Isabel's tendency to fit people into categories, is a third way in which essentialism is opposed.

Further opposition is registered, however faintly, by the suggested weakness, loneliness, and morbidity of the book's sublime essentialist, cousin Ralph, and also by the immense dislike the reader is encouraged to feel for the villain of the piece, Gilbert Osmond. Osmond is an essentialist insofar as he partakes of empty social ritual and conspicuous displays of aesthetic consumption solely to create in others a deceptive impression of what kind of man he is within. Isabel comes to despise her husband for this essentialism without seeming to recognize how much she too is obsessed with the impression she makes. Whereas Madame Merle claims (with whatever deceit in mind) that one's internal being is inseparable from one's external situation, Osmond, again like Isabel, clearly believes that external and internal are wholly separate. Manipulating the former does not, for him, change the latter but instead only regulates outsiders' interpretation.

At the level of story and characterization, the most important of the novel's internal subversions of its dominant ideology is wrapped up in Isabel. By its frequent reiteration that her suffering and the suffering she causes those who love her is the result of her naiveté, her unworldliness, her ignoring or not seeing the contradictions in people, the text suggests to the reader, though never strongly, that fixing human subjects and assigning them to conceptual categories inevitably invites disaster. Thus the text cautions against formalism applied to humans even though, by formalizing the humanlike agents who enact the narrative, it helps inculcate in its reader the same sort of behavior.

Isabel's Freedom: Henry James's *The Portrait of a Lady*

Maria Irene Ramalho de Sousa Santos

> *Das Gesetz hat noch keinen grossen Mann gebildet, aber die Freiheit brütet Kolosse und Extremitäten aus.*
>
> Karl Moor in *Die Räuber*

> *No, it is awful. She will be nobody's wife; she will be lost!*
>
> Darya Alexandrovna Oblonsky speaking of Anna Arkadyevna Karenin

> *The idea of the whole thing is that the poor girl, who has dreamed of freedom and nobleness . . . finds herself in reality ground in the very mill of the conventional.*
>
> HENRY JAMES speaking of Isabel Archer/Osmond

In an article that he very aptly called "The Moment of *The Portrait of a Lady*," Charles Feidelson shows how this novel represents not only a transitional point in James's work and thinking, but also a basic shift of fictional attitude in the nineteenth-century novel, moving towards the twentieth-century novel-of-consciousness. By placing "The centre of the subject in the young woman's own consciousness," James begins to reverse the whole idea of fictional narrative. While, for example, in *Bleak House* the social world around Esther Summerson defines her and even conditions her own narrative of herself, in *The Portrait of a Lady* it is Isabel's consciousness that *seems* to define and shape the world about her. Where before the novel had presented the characters in terms of the world—either in harmony with society or in opposition to it—now the novel begins to sketch the idea of a character that shapes the fictional form itself: the character-as-consciousness.

From *Biblos* 56 (1986). © 1980 by Irene Ramalho Santos.

From now on the world of fiction will depend more and more on the shaping power of this imagining consciousness. The main technical change is, then, a change of voice, or point of view. The so-called omniscient author—"the muffled majesty of authorship" James speaks of—no longer plays his former role. If the character's consciousness holds the center of interest, then the character's consciousness must "tell" the "story"; and "the artist, like the God of the creation, remains within or behind or beyond or above his handiwork, invisible, refined out of existence, indifferent, paring his fingernails" (James Joyce, *The Portrait of the Artist as a Young Man*). Although in *The Portrait,* and for that matter in James's work as a whole, we are still far from Joyce's radical stance of narrative absence, Henry James's novels must be read as transitional in this regard, and *The Portrait* as a clear turning point. Indeed, before we get to the hardly audible authorial voice in *The Golden Bowl,* we witness a process of gradual slowing down of the authoritative, supposedly knowledgeable narrative voice in *The Portrait,* until chapter 42, "the best thing in the book," the reader is left alone with the contemplation of Isabel, finally almost completely "translated" into the "formula" of her own consciousness.

Thus, from Dickens (or Jane Austen), where we have the individual concerned with society, to the extent that he or she depends on society for his or her own definition, we turn to James, where the individual becomes more and more preoccupied with his or her consciousness, to the extent that his or her alienation from society becomes the gauge of his or her identity. The Jamesian character, by his or her own introspective movement, begins seriously to question previous societal definitions and to assert the right to a separate identity. In this sense also, James's *Portrait* may still be said to be a social novel. For it depicts precisely this changing social context, or world system, in which an individual consciousness has lost its sense of an individual's defined place in the world, a sense of roots growing deeply in a solid soil, however menacing. If it is possible to say that James's deamericanized Americans are vivid dramatizations of this sense of displacement, the problem must not be seen merely in the light of James's International Theme. Lord Warburton, the preposterous radical aristocrat, is also definitely unable to reconcile his liberal ideology with the rigid form and the heavy weight of the English tradition in which he finds himself misplaced.

Isabel Archer seems to find her lack of place (or definition) the more interesting and appealing. She believes herself completely free to choose the absence of form that appears most congenial to her, thus typically neglecting the complex network of relationships in which individual facts

or events are rooted. Her love for an all-embracing (individual) consciousness equals her love of freedom. This is what is implied in [Richard] Chase's
view that "Isabel has higher ideals than any she thinks can be realized by
a life with Lord Warburton." Her higher ideals are the liberal ideals of a
"completed consciousness" and of individual freedom, whereas Lord Warburton, even if in spite of himself, has to offer only the "system" her
"instinct" tells her to "resist." It is clear right from the beginning of the
novel that Isabel Archer dreads the kind of definition implied in a commitment to what Lord Warburton represents, and that is why she cannot
"think of [his] various homes as the settled seat of [her] residence." She will
have to remain completely disengaged to pursue the "free exploration of
life" that her imagination dreams of.

This is exactly what she thinks she will begin to achieve when she
decides to marry Gilbert Osmond, the man who presents himself to her
seemingly without a system. In justifying her marital decision to Ralph,
Isabel says: "He [Osmond] wants me to know everything; that is what I
like him for"; and later on, still failing to see the intricate web of relationships, and resolutely ignoring Ralph's socializing warning that "one ought
to feel one's relation to things—to others," she refuses to see Osmond but
in the light of noble individuality and independence she bestows on him:
"He knows everything, he understands everything, he has the kindest,
gentlest, highest spirit." Thus, as she had rejected the social commitment
implicit in Lord Warburton's proposal, she now accepts the offer that seems
to her most uncommitted socially and that she believes to be the total
fulfilment of the freedom she needs to expand her imagination limitlessly:
"His being so independent, so individual, is what *I* most see in him."

Isabel believes, then, that her marriage to Osmond opens up for her
the broad road towards the complete fulfilment of her consciousness. Out
of that late-nineteenth-century, pre-war idealism that she, too, embodies,
Isabel cherishes the kind of individual freedom (i.e. disengagement, sepa-
rateness, independence) which she believes to be the essence of human
consciousness. So, in freedom as she thinks, she chooses to marry the man
that had seemed to her most uncommitted, most unconcerned, most disinterested, most independent, most free. Thus, Isabel will truly find herself,
as a woman, in her marriage, which is no less than the symbolic reconciliation of her notion of freedom with society's (and her own) as yet un-
questioned definition of woman as somebody's wife.

Up to this point we have the social novel about how bad or how good
a marriage a certain intelligent and idealistic, but rather presumptuously
independent young girl will make. *The Portrait of a Lady* begins overtly like

a comedy of manners, with its beautiful Gardencourt setting of English amenities and afternoon tea. Like Jane Austen's heroines, Isabel Archer is also mainly concerned with the difficult problem of marriage. The main issue in the first part of the book seems to be how Isabel will fit in the events that surround her, or rather, how she will attain that important goal of all Austen's heroines: appropriate *location* in a surrounding society by means of a suitable marriage. For in this society, as in Tolstoy's tzarist Russia, to be nobody's wife is to be lost indeed. However, little by little the reader begins to realize that, unlike what happens in Austen's novels, the interesting thing about Isabel is not how she will eventually fit in the surrounding events, but rather if and how the events fit *her*. Since we shall find out in the end that the events in the novel do not fit its heroine at all, that she will rather have to re-invent her freedom in order to force herself to fit them, the *moment* of *The Portrait of a Lady* turns out to be more telling than a mere technical change of fictional stances. While in earlier novels of manners and social comedy the center of interest lay mainly on the full definition of womanhood within society by a woman's right (or wrong) choice of marriage, in *The Portrait* the center of interest is gradually shifting from social events to the main character's consciousness; and marriage, rightly or wrongly assumed, is being quietly, perhaps inadvertently, put into question as a woman's defining principle.

For Feidelson's argument it is indeed important to emphasize the word *consciousness* in James's much quoted piece of self-advice, "Place the center of the subject in the young woman's consciousness"; but the fact that the consciousness is that of a young *woman's* must never slip out of one's mind. Like Hawthorne's *The Scarlet Letter* or George Eliot's *Middlemarch,* two obvious predecessors of *The Portrait,* or James's own short novel *Daisy Miller, The Portrait of a Lady* reflects its author's latent social preoccupations, or his sensitivity to the changing times, precisely in his heroine's quest for freedom, i.e. in her control, or lack of control, of her own destiny. Whether James actually wanted it so or not, by implicitly siding with many other nineteenth-century authors in their concern for the woman's place in society, James made of Isabel's consciousness not just the growing consciousness of a presumptuous girl, around whom an ado is organized, but the very arena upon which the structure of society is questioned through the young woman's "searching [self-] criticism."

The novel-of-consciousness in *The Portrait* begins, therefore, when Isabel sits down to *think* of what has happened to her consciousness and to her freedom; it begins when Isabel learns how to make connections and relate events; it begins when her thoughtful self-criticism enlightens her as to the calculated intrigues that had necessitated her marriage. Isabel's discoveries about her freedom or lack of freedom, as well as her final stubborn attempt to mend the broken image of her illusion of self-control, must then also be read as an implicit comment on the shifting values of the late nineteenth century, such as individualism and individual freedom, integrity and dignity of mind and consciousness, inner authenticity and coherence in absolute terms (i.e. regardless of external, social circumstances). Isabel's self-probing consciousness, as well as the subtle gradual translation of social comedy into the novel-of-consciousness, are already clear signs of the crisis in western thinking and ideals that Fredric Jameson has called "the bankruptcy of the liberal tradition." In James's world, independent young women either die, like Daisy Miller, or, like Isabel Archer/Osmond, are mercilessly crushed by a conventional form. In the following attempt to explain once again why Isabel Archer returns to Rome and to her husband at the end of the novel, I suggest that James's heroine is desperately trying to preserve a lost ideal of individual freedom as the basis for a woman's social identity.

II

> Isabel sat there looking up at her, without rising; her face almost a prayer to be enlightened. But the light of this woman's eyes seemed only a darkness. "O misery!" she murmured at last; and she fell back, covering her face with her hands. It had come over her like a high surging wave that Mrs. Touchett was right. Madame Merle had married her. Before she uncovered her face again that lady had left the room.

In his Notebook entry on *The Portrait of a Lady,* Henry James was still debating whether he should have Madame Merle or the Countess Gemini break the news to Isabel about Madame Merle's relationship to Pansy and Osmond. He thinks that it would be "better on many grounds" that it should be the Countess, and yet he regrets to have, in that case, to lose "the 'great scene' between Madame Merle and Isabel." The passage I quoted above shows how James was able to have the Countess be messenger of bad news and still save one "great scene" between Madame Merle and Isabel. The scene is indeed great. It is a crucial scene in the whole novel, particularly important for our understanding of Isabel's sense of freedom, and her subsequent attempts to preserve it. Isabel Osmond—trapped by the calculated machinations of her husband and of Madame Merle—begins to realize how far away she is now from Isabel Archer, the independent young woman at the beginning of the novel, a symbol in herself of unlimited freedom in her latent potentialities.

After this momentous interview with Madame Merle, Isabel has to go out into the open air: "she wished to be far away, under the sky, where she could descend from her carriage and tread upon the daisies." Of course, this had already become a habit with her. The weariness accumulated in "the house of darkness, the house of dumbness, the house of suffocation" she would rest "upon things that had crumbled for centuries and yet still were upright." It was relieving and refreshing to identify her own sense of wreckage and desolation with the dismal, pain-echoing ruins of the grandeur that Rome had been. The image of a glorious decadence around her worked like a balsamic consolation on her battered, and yet still dignified soul. This time, however, it seems that Isabel's impulse to run into the open space of the Roman landscape comes mainly as a result of her sudden confrontation with the overwhelming revelation: the most important decision of her life had been determined, not by her own free choice, but by someone else's deliberate calculations. In freedom she had wanted to be enlightened, and in bondage she had received only the most terrifying darkness. She had wished her consciousness to expand itself into the realm of beauty in its completeness, and finds out, abjectly, that what she believes to be the basic presupposition for human consciousness itself—freedom—had been lacking in her all the time. The openness of space between the daisies and the sky will help create around her, outside her, the illusion of the liberty she is miserably missing inside her.

We shall have to recapitulate what things like freedom, and liberty, and independence, and self-confidence had always meant to Isabel to understand all the implications of such a discovery. Our first glimpse of Isabel is that telegraphic "quite independent," which Mrs. Touchett had considered an important piece of information to include in her scanty message to her family. When Isabel herself appears on the lawn of Gardencourt, she strikes Ralph as having "a great deal of confidence, both in herself and in others." A little later, she will be appalled at the very idea of being considered "a candidate for adoption": "I'm very fond of my liberty," she says. Liberty means to know everything, including all the possibilities ahead in order to choose freely, confidently, responsibly; as when she tells her aunt that she always likes to know the things one shouldn't do, "so as to choose." A few pages later, we find Isabel afraid of becoming "a mere sheep in the flock"; she wants to be the sole free master of her own fate. In other words, Isabel declines to be a puppet; she wants to act always within the limits of human dignity, which she measures by the freedom of human consciousness.

These are, of course, some of the romantic "theories" of "the mere slim shade of an intelligent but presumptuous girl." When she apparently becomes really free to "meet the requirements of [her] imagination," Isabel is intuitively afraid. Unaware of the liberal fallacy of her notion of individual freedom, regardless of the complex interactions at work in human society, Isabel is, however, perceptive enough to sense the trap she may be walking into: "A large fortune means freedom, and I'm afraid of that." Isabel is right to be afraid, for indeed her desire for total freedom will eventually have to be translated into freedom-as-accepted-necessity. I shall come back to this. Meanwhile, Isabel's new fortune brings her an enlarged freedom, however problematic. She believes herself now to be freer than ever before, and she thinks that, from now on, she will have to cope with a boundless imagination. She is scared of the burden of tremendous responsibility involved in complete, unquestionable freedom, but she is also exhilarated at the thought of her consciousness opening up, infinitely, towards the fulfilment of its own potentialities. That her love of freedom equals her fear of freedom is only an indication of changing values and conceptions in James's own world: liberal individualism, all too questionably presented in Isabel's portrait—she is anxious about the use she will make of her freedom, but she never doubts its reality; she believes herself to be in complete control of her destiny. She is free—she thinks—to choose her own fate. And so she believes she does when she fulfills her "one ambition—to be free to follow out a good feeling." For a person like Isabel, to whom this kind of liberty had always been the dearest, most cherished value of human life, how dreadful and how crushing and how destructive Madame Merle's revelation must have been! No wonder Isabel had to go out into the open air to try to rescue herself from total suffocation.

In marrying Osmond, as she thinks, in freedom, Isabel had wanted "to transfer the weight [of her money] to some other conscience, to some more prepared receptacle." That is, she had wanted to share her liberty with a freer, unprejudiced consciousness, which she hoped to be the fulfilment of her own. Her marriage had then been for her the symbol of her total freedom. When Isabel becomes gradually aware of her error of perception concerning Osmond's character—that though she had married *in* freedom, she had *not married freedom*—all her strength and sense of dignity come to her through her still, and now ever more, cherished ideal of freedom as opposed to her husband's strict conformity to standard traditions or sterile forms:

> Her notion of the aristocratic life was simply the union of great
> knowledge with great liberty. . . . But for Osmond it was al-
> together a thing of forms, a conscious calculated attitude. He
> was fond of the old, the consecrated, the transmitted; so was
> she, but she pretended to do what she chose with it.

The belief that she is free, has always been, and still is, in spite of the rigid system that Osmond wants to close about her, saves Isabel somehow from irrevocable spiritual death. She had made a mistake, she knows; but she believes she had been free to make it, and that belief saves her self-respect for her. Her sense of freedom is now the only glimmering light in the darkness of her habitation, a quiet, obstinate preservation of integrity, that reflects itself fundamentally in her passive-resistance-like attitude towards Ralph.

Up to the famous scene between Isabel and Madame Merle in chapter 49, two forceful motives have been keeping Isabel faithful to the sacred ideal of her marriage. First, she had been free when she had decided to marry Gilbert Osmond, and therefore she feels she must accept the consequences of her acts, however painful: "one must accept one's deeds. I married him before all the world; I was perfectly free; it was impossible to do anything more deliberate." Secondly, as Henrietta rightly points out in this passage, Isabel's pride determines her unwillingness to admit that she has made a mistake. She knows that she has made a mistake, but she cannot publish it: "I don't think that's decent. I'd much rather die." Isabel's attitude need not, indeed must not be understood merely as the vain stubbornness of a foolish presumptuous girl who stupidly refuses to admit that she has made a mistake; it is rather, in a way, a privilege of her sense of freedom; she is still free to chose the face she wants to show, and she chooses *not* to acknowledge *publicly* such a gross error of perception on her part concerning Osmond. As she tells Henrietta, she owes that much to her own respect for such liberal, Emersonian values as she was taught to love: individual freedom, self-reliance, self-responsibility.

However, there is surely a certain naiveté and immaturity in Isabel's desperate need "to feel that her unhappiness should not have come to her through her own fault." In the very first draft of Isabel's portrait, we learn that "she had an infinite hope that she should never do anything wrong," we learn how much she dreads "inconsistency" and "hollowness," and how much she would like "to find herself some day in a difficult position, so that she should have the pleasure of being as heroic as the occasion demanded." In other words, Isabel Archer had always been anxious about the use she would ever make of her freedom, which she never doubts or questions, and her deepest wish had always been ever *to do right*. So that, when she finds herself, as Ralph had foreseen, "in trouble," her first thought goes to a justification of herself. The "need to right herself" that worries Isabel at the beginning of the novel has now gained a deeper meaning for her. In accepting the consequences of what she believes to have been her free acts. Isabel is again in possession of the satisfaction of "doing herself justice," of doing herself the justice of being considerate of herself, of being after all as heroic as the difficulty of the situation demanded. Once, as she thinks, "the sole source of her mistake had been within herself," in order to keep the sense of her dignity in her own eyes, Isabel has to assume the burden of her initial error. This is justification before herself; before others, her pride prevents her from even admitting her mistake. She is free; she may therefore choose to go on showing the world the *image* of her freedom. Thus, while she knows that "the place has surrendered," she wants her flag to be seen waving high up in the sky.

And yet, suddenly, Isabel lets her flag drop. She has to. When she finds out how little free she had been in the most important decision of her life, how much she had been made a convenience of, Isabel is wretchedly confronted with her own collapsing dignity as a human being. Freedom is the highest value, the sum of all human dignity. The discovery of Madame Merle's and Osmond's interference in her marriage forces Isabel to see herself as a mere instrument, a useful tool in other people's hands, a mere puppet. This might have been a comfortable discovery for someone who had wished ever to do right. But Isabel's subsequent behavior indicates that she loves individual freedom more than she loves self-righteousness. If Isabel's discovery washes white the guilt and responsibility of her misery, it also deprives her, to her mind, of human dignity and tragic stature. There is only one gesture left for Isabel: *to invest with freedom,* retrospectively, her initially determined, conditioned choice. Thus, in sanctioning her first act, in turning it, retroactively, into a free act, Isabel finally *creates* (or invents?) her real freedom, the liberty of fully expanded consciousness, backwards and forwards, in complete, calculating control of itself. That the gesture is merely a symbolic one, and that Isabel's *willed* freedom—ominously reminiscent of Emerson's "terrible freedom" inside—is now unequivocally an *image* of freedom, again points to the novel's subtle problematization of late-nineteenth-century values.

The interpreter might argue that Isabel would not have been less free or responsible if she had decided to turn away from Osmond and Rome; but Isabel's idealistic humanism had taught her a different lesson. Her notion

of human freedom, dignity, and responsibility, as well as her ideal of marriage and her conception of a woman's place in society, inexorably trace
for her, paradoxically, her freely chosen path, To be free, then, is to be
master of one's destiny. That Isabel achieves by her retrospective act; but
she is nonetheless trapped in her disengaged ideals and, as a woman, double
trapped. As she confides to Ralph right before he dies, her final decision
will be dictated by what "seems right." To ratify retroactively her initial
choice of fate had meant to choose her destiny again, to redefine her marriage
as freedom fulfilled, to assume her identity as Mrs. Osmond, without which
she would now be lost. Thus, although the interpreter might say that, in
wanting to ascend towards the realm of ends, Isabel is most vilely trapped
in the world of means, Isabel herself, by her ratifying act, finds herself
finally soaring above a world of necessity and dependence. Seemingly returning to the darkness and dumbness of her suffocating habitation, she is
indeed at last enjoying for the first time the meaning of a free, responsible
consciousness. How heroic and noble this is will depend, of course, on the
value one attributes to Isabel's idea of freedom and responsibility. What I
mean is that it may still be difficult for many of us in this day and age to
see Oedipus as a mere plaything in the hands of the gods of iron necessity.
We demand some sense of freedom, guilt, and responsibility in order to
grasp the magnificent dignity of the king's tragedy. This may seem too
much of an ado about Isabel Archer; but wasn't exactly that James's idea,
that of "organizing an ado about Isabel Archer"?

I therefore suggest that Isabel's final decision to go back to her husband,
in *enfranchising* her first choice, endows her with the responsibility one
demands of all free human beings. When in the end she rejects Caspar
Goodwood's proposal, though of course the motive of sexual fear is very
obvious, Isabel is above all aware that Caspar's idea of freedom is at odds
with her own, that it would indeed nullify her very conception of herself.
For Goodwood, freedom means "that a woman deliberately made to suffer
is justified in anything in life"; for Isabel, freedom means that a woman
that has made herself responsible for her own suffering has only "one
straight path" to follow: the wide, but painful, path of authenticity. For
the first time in her life, Isabel may be said to be truly, knowingly consistent.
Or, as the observant Ralph [James?] might have said, she is once and for
all "dismally consistent."

A brief digression will help me put James's novel and its ideals and
values, particularly its problematical conception of freedom, in the broader
context of Western Literature. At the beginning of Shiller's *Die Räuber,*
young Karl Moor expresses his titanic, Promethean longing for glorious

deeds that are only to be achieved in freedom: "Das Gesetz hat noch keinen grossen Mann gebildet, aber die Freiheit brütet Kolosse und Extremitäten aus." A deep loathing for the sickly, corrupt laws of mankind turns Moor into an outcast and a robber. When later he finds out that his is not the task, nor the right, to chastise mankind in the name of a higher moral order, it is loo late to retrieve. Moor has now lost Shiller's highest values: his freedom and the purity of his conscience. The oath sworn among the robbers and their leader binds Karl Moor helplessly to the iron chain of his band, necessity drags him down forcefully, step by step, towards destruction and self-annihilation. Only when in the end Moor recognizes the higher value of divine and human law does he become free again. Moor had dared to assume as a right of his own the task of purifying a polluted mankind, failing to realize that in breaking the law he was shaking the very moral grounds of the world. When finally he is horrified to think that "zwei Menschen wie ich den ganzen Bau der sittlichen Welt zugrund richten würden," Karl Moor understands that man's freedom lies deep within the boundaries of law. He therefore shuns the pseudo-freedom of suicide (cf. Isabel's death wish at the end of the novel), as he had just rejected the pseudo-freedom of lawlessness. Liberty is wilful acceptance of law itself (cf. Isabel's wilful acceptance of her *lawful* marriage), as the only safeguard of the world's and man's order. This is the only freedom, Schiller suggests, that makes giants of men.

In drawing the parallel between *Die Räuber* and *The Portrait of a Lady*, one has, of course, to be discriminating. Karl Moor is deeply concerned with the destiny of mankind, whereas Isabel is mainly concerned with what happens to her own consciousness. The difference lies surely on the different social and cultural contexts that helped create both works, and it may also be seen as an indication of the growing fictional concern with the human consciousness as a subject. Karl Moor's attitude in the end shows how much the order of the world depends on the freedom of human consciousness to accept legal restraint. In *The Portrait of a Lady* the process is somehow reversed: the integrity (or order) of Isabel's consciousness depends entirely on her free acceptance of the "mill of the conventional," in order to secure her threatened liberty. But while Karl Moor, in accepting *Gesetz* as a higher *Freiheit*, is admitting how conditioned by necessity his past life had been, Isabel's return to Rome, as I read it, is a choice of freedom *in the past:* her gesture ratifies her first decision to marry Osmond, which now becomes truly a free decision. In returning to Rome, Isabel sets herself free, retrospectively, and she is thus as responsible for her deeds as becomes a tragic figure. On the other hand, at the very bottom of both Isabel's and Moor's motivation, we may discern an unconfessed desire for self-glorification. After all, if Isabel Archer had always been longing for some heroic deed in her life, perhaps the accusation of Karl Moor's fellow-robber in the end is not entirely false either: "Lasst ihn hinfahren! Es ist die Grossmannsucht. Er will sein Leben an eitle Bewunderung setzen." So that Isabel is as much the author of her "*tragedy* of consciousness" as Karl Moor is the victim of his own tragedy of freedom.

I would not assert, *positively,* that James wanted to give Isabel a tragic dimension; but I do wish to suggest that he wanted *her* to give *herself* a tragic dimension. In so constructing a new sense of freedom, Isabel was indeed acting as heroically, or as tragically, as the occasion demanded. We are not only beholding "a kind of inverted triumph" instead of "the waste and degradation of a splendid spirit," as Arnold Kettle says; we are also looking at the last masterly touch on Isabel's ideal portrait of herself as a wholly liberated consciousness. That the symbol of her liberation is her sterile marriage must be understood, I think, as an indication of James's implied criticism of her ideals.

I do not want to turn Isabel's conquest of freedom into the sole motive for her return to Rome. She has plenty of reasons to take that decision, as a perfunctory glimpse at the secondary literature would assure us. There is, to name but a few, Isabel's conception of marriage as "sacred": her fear of sexual passion as offered by Goodwood's alternative; Isabel's promise to Pansy not to "desert" her; her dread of public exposure; her respect for "certain obligations . . . involved in the very fact of marriage." However, the reader is made to sense, in the course of the last chapters of the novel, that none of these reasons is sufficient. Isabel seems all too anxious to find a new reason to return to Rome when the previous one proves no longer valid. Her fear of Goodwood's aggressive manhood at the very end doesn't seem to be enough good reason, either, for, after all, she not only escapes from him but also *does* return to Rome. The last scene between these two characters strikes me rather as one more symbolic aspect of Isabel's desperate quest for freedom. "Why should you go through that ghastly form?" Goodwood asks her; and Isabel replies, "to get away from *you.*" If Caspar may be said to stand here for the world that considers Isabel guiltless of her mistake, it is in his eyes that Isabel must more than ever justify herself as a free human being, always in command of her fate, always responsible for her life. If she should for a moment allow herself to suspect that her marriage—i.e. that which alone gives her (social) identity—is at odds with her ideal of freedom, she would be lost indeed.

To conclude I should like to go back to James's preface and then comment a little on the novel's inconclusive closure. Says James:

The obvious criticism of course will be that it is not finished—
that I have not seen the heroine to the end of her situation—that
I have left her *en l'air*—this is both true and false. The *whole* of
anything is never told; you can only take what groups together.
What I have done has that unity—it groups together. It is complete in itself—and the rest may be taken up or not, later.

James is here clearly toying with the idea that *The Portrait of a Lady* is not
the end of Isabel's story and I will knowingly bite the bait and rather commit
the crime of meaningful speculation than that of sterile synchronicity. Isabel's story is not only the story of a woman's changing place in society,
but also the very chronicle of society itself. That the only noble and dignified
way that Isabel has of refusing to be "ground in the . . . mill of the conventional" is to accept the "ghastly form" knowingly and freely, is a telling
comment on the kind of society presented in James's world; and a comment,
too, on the kind of (American) literary tradition this international novelist
feeds on: Isabel Archer/Osmond is undoubtedly a lesser Hester Prynne, but
still a potential "rebel" who willingly accepts the role of an "agent of
socialization." The time has obviously not yet come for the fulfilment of
Hester Prynne's ambiguous prophecy at the end of *The Scarlet Letter:*

at some brighter period, when the world should have grown
ripe for it, in Heaven's own time, a new truth would be revealed,
in order to establish the whole relation between man and woman
on a surer ground of mutual happiness.

However, the choice of a woman's growing consciousness for the portrayal
of a changing awareness of society's inconsistencies and incongruities is
surely an indication that James, in questioning isolated conceptions and
values and in drawing attention to their interrelation and interdependence
in their large societal context, is indeed reformulating in a newer light Hester
Prynne's implied conviction that a critique of society must begin with a
searching critique of the relation between man and woman, not in "Heaven's
own time," but right *now,* in the time of undeniable social reality—a deep
reaching critique of "the bottomless idiocy of the world."

""Understanding Allegories": Reading *The Portrait of a Lady*

Deborah Esch

> *To read between the lines was easier than to follow the text.*
> HENRY JAMES, *The Portrait of a Lady*

Ever a vigilant critic of his own work as well as that of other writers, James frequently took occasion in his essays and prefaces to remark on the exigencies of what was for him "the most difficult, the most delicate," "the most complicated and the most particular" of the arts. In "The Science of Criticism," written for the *New Review* in May 1891, and reprinted in 1893 under the abbreviated title "Criticism," he reflected on the intellectual and affective "outfit" required for work in the critical spirit, and granted that

> one is ready to pay almost any homage to the intelligence that has put it on; and when one considers the noble figure completely equipped—armed *cap à pie* in curiosity and sympathy—one falls in love with the apparition. It certainly represents the knight who has knelt through his long vigil and who has the piety of his office.

The essay pursues the metaphor of the vigil, and in its closing line supplies a further analogy for the activity of criticism:

> Any vocation has its hours of intensity that is so closely connected with life. That of the critic, in literature, is connected doubly, for he deals with life at second-hand as well as at first; that is, he deals with the experience of others, which he resolves

---

into his own, and not of those invented and selected others with whom the novelist makes comfortable terms, but with the uncompromising swarm of authors, the clamorous children of history. . . . We must be easy with him if the picture, even when the aim has really been to penetrate, is sometimes confused, for there are baffling and there are thankless subjects; and we make everything up to him by the peculiar purity of our esteem when the portrait is really, like the happy portraits of the other art, a text preserved by translation.

The analogy with the "other art," like the earlier metaphor of the vigil, directs the reader of these reflections to *The Portrait of a Lady*. Isabel Archer, the lady imaged in the titular portrait, proves to be "connected doubly" with criticism, in a doubleness signalled in the pivotal genitive of the novel's title: she is arguably its object—its text—as well as its subject—its reader. In the first extended account of his heroine in the novel's sixth chapter, *The Portrait*'s narrator caps a catalogue of her virtues and flaws with the observation that "she would be an easy victim of scientific criticism if she were not intended to awaken on the reader's part an impulse more tender and more purely expectant." In these terms, echoed elsewhere in the novel, Isabel figures the text, and her "portrait" becomes, according to the analogy of the essay on criticism, more precisely a text preserved by translation. On the other hand, in the chapter singled out by James in the preface to *The Portrait* as "obviously the best thing in the book," and "a supreme illustration of the general plan," Isabel herself takes up the "extraordinary meditative vigil," the "vigil of searching criticism." What Richard Poirier, in an account of the heroine as a figure for the author, represents as Isabel's "whole effort at self-creation, the impulse which makes her into a kind of novelist of her own experience," in James's terms culminates in the lady's assuming the stance of the critical "knight" of his own analogy—the position of a vigilant reader attempting to interpret a text—in this case, the text of her own past. Isabel's "hours of intensity" by the dying fire in chapter 42 attest to her critical vocation, baffling and thankless as it proves. To trace the consequences of her "double connection" to criticism, to mark its rhythm of alternation in the novel, is, for James's reader, to begin to account for the complexity of the "portraiture" in question.

The "Portrait" as Text in Translation

It is in the context of "the critical question," and in particular the question of "self-criticism," that James puts forward the well-known analogy between his own project of revision for the New York edition of his works, and the methods of the painter. In the first of the critical prefaces, that to *Roderick Hudson,* he writes of the "subject" he shares with the visual artist: "the painter's subject consisting ever, obviously, of the related state, to each other, of certain figures and things" (*The Art of the Novel*). James reactivates the analogy later in the preface to convey his sense of the labor of revision, the memory-work of "living back," of "taking up the old relation":

> I speak of the painter in general and of his relation to the old picture, the work of his hand, that has been lost to sight and that, when found again, is put back on the easel for measure of what time and the weather may, in the interval, have done to it. . . . The anxious artist has to wipe it over, in the first place, to see; he has to "clean it up," say, or to varnish it anew, or at the least to place it in a light, for any right judgement of its aspect or its worth.

The painterly analogy, then, arises with respect to the art of composition, but finds its fullest expression in the author's account of the actively critical practice of revision: "The painter who passes over his old sunk canvas the wet sponge that shows him what may still come out again makes his criticism essentially active." What James designates in this early preface as "the simplest figure for my revision of this present array of earlier, later, larger, smaller canvases" is noted and elaborated in turn by F. O. Matthiessen in his influential essay "The Painter's Sponge and Varnish Bottle," an analysis of James's emendations of and additions to *The Portrait of a Lady*.

While the contour of Isabel Archer's history as it emerges from the narrative sequence of the novel is manifestly irreducible to the instantaneity of a visual representation, critics of *The Portrait* have nonetheless followed Matthiessen's lead (and James's) in their enthusiastic adoption of the vocabulary of painting for their own interpretive accounts of the work. In the introduction to his edition of the novel, Leon Edel adheres scrupulously to the terms of that analogy: he writes of the text as "an imposing canvas of an American woman," hung by the artist in "the great gallery of the world's fiction." Edel is able to reproduce his vision of the portrait in graphic detail in the closing paragraph of his introduction:

> This book, then, is the portrait of a young American lady of great innocence and of high spirit which Henry James placed many years ago in the gallery of the novel. She is seated in the

picture. Her clasped hands are in repose; they rest in the lap of her black dress. She looks out at us with her light grey eyes, and her face, framed by her black hair, is one of rare beauty. Although she holds her head high and sits erect, there is something flexible about her, suggesting she can turn this way and that in her alertness. . . . She is beautifully painted; every touch of the artist's brush has been lovingly applied to this descendant of the Puritans who, from her highly-varnished surface, looks down at us always with the freshness of her spirit and the presumption of her youth.

There is something unsettling in this suggestion of the possibility that the portrait can move, indicated late in the novel in the "awful simile" that expresses Pansy Osmond's nameless dread: "Her heart may have stood almost as still as it would have done had she seen two of the saints in the great picture in the convent-chapel turn their painted heads and *shake them at each other*" (emphasis added). If the biographer, despite the decidedly negative inscription into the text itself of the gesture he attributes to the canvas, is able nonetheless to render the portrait in such detail, it may be due to his appeal outside the novel for a model for James's heroine. Edel cites the resemblance, noted by friends of the author, between Isabel Archer and his cousin Minny Temple, who (like Isabel's cousin Ralph Touchett) succumbed to tuberculosis at the age of twenty-four. Though Edel quotes it in support of his thesis, James's reply to his friend Grace Norton, who wrote him of her recognition of the likeness, suggests that to refer Isabel to this "original" on the basis of a perceived resemblance is, while understandable, also mistaken, in instructive and symptomatic ways: "You are both right and wrong about Minny Temple. I had her in my mind and there is in the heroine a considerable infusion of my impression of her remarkable nature. But the thing is not a portrait. Poor Minny was essentially *incomplete* and I have attempted to make my young woman more rounded, more finished."

It seems that despite James's appeal to visual representation in the title of the novel and in his own critical writings, and despite the good will of his interpreters in taking him at his word, *The Portrait* is, in a sense yet to be determined, *not* a portrait. James's flatly negative claim is most immediately that the novel is not strictly mimetic, a faithful and complete rendering from life—in other words, that it does not appeal finally to a particular and specifiable extra-textual object as its referent. But to deny that *The Portrait* is a portrait in not only to indicate the limitations of the static (*pace* Edel) and instantaneous visual metaphor for the interpretation of sequential narratives. It is as well to question whether the novel's spectrum of significations includes a referential moment of the same order as that constitutive of the art of portraiture. The logic by which Grace Norton (and Edel) can be "both right and wrong" about the relation between Isabel Archer and Minny Temple—the referential moment being finally inevitable (and to that extent "right"), but "wrong" when understood in strictly mimetic terms—is the same as the logic that allows James to claim that *The Portrait* is not a portrait. In question is not a mere negation (such as would be expressed in the claim "A text is not a portrait"), but rather a double-bind in which the self-identity of the portrait—and the text—is in doubt.

A provisional response to this question of referentiality is suggested in the closing simile of "The Science of Criticism," cited earlier, which converts the metaphor of the "happy portrait"—a figure for successful criticism—to that of a text, and specifically "a text preserved by translation." The latter figure supplies the temporal dimension (that of "preservation") as well as the sense of textuality missing from the comparison with visual representation. It specifies further that the text in question is not, despite claims to the contrary on the part of its admirers, an "original," but is readable only at the interlinguistic remove of a (figurative) translation.

In *The Portrait's* preface, James associates the activity of translation with the "technical rigour" of composition, and in particular with the task of establishing the "figure" of his heroine in the context of her "relations": "The girl hovers, indistinguishable, as a charming creature, and the job will be to translate her into the highest terms of that formula, and as nearly as possible moreover into *all* of them." The inconspicuous deployment of the metaphor of translation in this context arguably governs a set of concerns raised in the preface, generally grouped by critics (e.g. Krook and Blackmur) under the rubric of the "international theme," and enacted historically in the "simultaneous 'serialization' of the novel in the two countries that the changing conditions of literary intercourse between England and the United States had up to then left unaltered." Moreover, unlike the other notable metaphors in the preface, particularly the much remarked "house of fiction" and the accompanying architectural figures, the trope of translation in consistent with a system of figuration associated in the novel itself with its protagonist. The marked "originality" repeatedly attributed to Isabel is figured from early in the narrative in specifically textual terms, notably in an exchange in chapter 4 between her brother-in-law and his wife, Lilian, of whom the narrator attests that "the two things in life of which she was most distinctly conscious were her husband's force in argument and her sister Isabel's originality." Her preoccupations converge when Mr. Ludlow's argumentative force is brought to bear on Lilian's insistence upon Isabel's originality:

> "Well, I don't like originals; I like translations," Mr. Ludlow had more than once replied. "Isabel's written in a foreign tongue. I can't make her out. She ought to marry an Armenian or a Portuguese."
>
> "That's just what I'm afraid she'll do!" cried Lilian, who thought her sister capable of anything.

Edmund Ludlow, who has "always thought Isabel rather foreign," registers her originality as that of a text that requires translation into the mother tongue in order to be understood (like the "German name" of the convent's drawing master, which, in the view of one of the nuns, "needed to be translated" into Italian before it can be communicated to Osmond). If Lilian fails to understand her sister's originality in these terms, hers is not the most consequential error of its kind. We are subsequently reminded that Gilbert Osmond "was fond of originals, of rarities, of the superior and the exquisite"; when he learns of Isabel's rejection of Lord Warburton's marriage proposal, "he perceived a new attraction in the idea of taking to himself a young lady who had qualified herself to figure in his collection of choice objects by declining so noble a hand." Osmond misreads the terms of Isabel's figurative originality in a characteristic gesture that does not so much domesticate her foreignness as it aestheticizes her textuality—and the upshot of his error is readable in subsequent chapters. Ralph Touchett's sense of Isabel's originality is less reductive, though his terms of comparison are likewise aesthetic: while he distinguishes her as "finer than the finest work of art—than a Greek bas-relief, than a great Titian, than a Gothic cathedral," his conclusion that "Isabel's originality was that she gave one an impression of having intentions of her own" is more suggestive. Isabel (who, we are told, is "reported to have read the classic authors—in translation"), for her part, fails initially to understand the order of Osmond's own originality: "Her mind contained no class offering a natural place to Mr. Osmond—he was a specimen apart . . . he indulged in no deflections from common usage, he was an original without being an eccentric." On the other hand, her reading of Madame Merle's "bold, free invention" is from the first resolutely textual: "Madame Merle was not superficial—not she. She was deep, and her nature spoke none the less in her behaviour because it spoke a conventional tongue. 'What's language at all but a convention?' said Isabel. 'She has the good taste not to pretend, like some people I've met, to express herself by original signs.' "

Despite her sister's fears and her brother-in-law's prescriptions, Isabel marries neither an Armenian nor a Portuguese, nor even a British nobleman, but instead a displaced American permanently transplanted to Italy. The Atlantic crossing that eventually lands Isabel in Rome becomes, on the eve of her acceptance of Osmond, the portentous figure of "a last vague space" that her imagination "couldn't cross—a dusky, uncertain tract which looked ambiguous and even slightly treacherous. . . . But she was to cross it yet." Isabel's eventual crossing is also readable as the span inscribed in translation itself (as well as in metaphor, whose "literal" sense is "to carry over, across"). (A span that is also temporal, as will be suggested in what follows.) An historic analogue is afforded in the migration of language that James recounts in "The Question of Our Speech," a lecture addressed to the graduating class at Bryn Mawr College in June 1905. He there reminds his audience of what he himself "cannot wholly forget," namely

> that the adventure, as I name it, of our idiom and the adventure of our utterance have been fundamentally the same adventure and the same experience; that they at a given period migrated together, immigrated together, into the great raw world in which they were to be cold-shouldered and neglected together, left to run wild and lose their way together.

He exhorts the graduates to

> keep in sight the so interesting historical truth that no language, so far back as our acquaintance with history goes, has known any such ordeal, any such stress and strain, as was to await the English in this huge new community it was so unsuspectingly to help, at first, to father and mother. It came *over*, as the phrase is, came over originally, without fear and without guile—but to find itself transplanted to spaces it had never dreamed, in its comparative innocence, of meeting.

While the crossing of the English idiom and utterance to America runs chiastically counter to Isabel Archer's migration to England, both "came *over* . . . originally, without fear and without guile," to meet fates they could not have anticipated. Indeed, the English language becomes, in James's idiosyncratic rendering of "this chapter in its history," itself the friendless heroine (in keeping with the gender conventionally assigned to the "mother tongue") of an adventure:

Taken on the whole by surprise it may doubtless be said to have behaved as well as unfriended heroine ever behaved in dire predicament—refusing, that is, to be frightened quite to death, looking about for a *modus vivendi,* consenting to live, preparing to wait on developments. I say "unfriended" heroine because that is exactly my point: that whereas the great idioms of Europe in general have grown up at home and in the family, the ancestral circle (with their migrations all comfortably prehistoric), our medium of utterance was to be disjoined from all the associations, the other presences, that had attended her, that had watched for her and with her, that had helped to form her manners and her voice, her taste and her genius.

The translation that takes place in this account thus winds up as a disarticulation, a "disjoining" of the "medium of utterance" from attendant associations and presences. With respect to Isabel's own "dire predicament" (and in light of her final willed isolation, a self-imposed disjunction from friends and allies), another analogy thus suggests itself: that between translation and matrimony, which turn mutually around the question of a contractual commitment to fidelity that is inevitably tested and readily broken. (Cf. in this context Ralph Touchett's contention that "it was of the essence of marriage to be open to criticism.") The question then becomes whether Isabel's first and final fidelity to Osmond, which dismays most of the novel's critics only slightly less than it does Caspar Goodwood, is duly enacted on the level of language. If Isabel's "originality" requires translation in order to be understood, and if, in keeping with the analogy with marriage, that translation must be faithful, what does such fidelity entail? And how is it to be reconciled with Isabel's other marked attribute, in evidence from first to last—her "fondness" for her "freedom"? How, finally, is the critical reader of the text to avoid the metaphorical bind of Ralph Touchett (who is said to possess, in the form of a Harvard and Oxford education, the "key to modern criticism", for whom "living as he now lived was like reading a good book in a poor translation—a meagre entertainment for a young man who felt that he might have been an excellent linguist"?

The simplest notion of a faithful or "true" translation is that of a transparent and adequate interexpression, and the guage of adequacy, of fidelity to the original has conventionally been the successful conveyance, to the reader's understanding, of its meaning. "Faithfulness to the text has meant faithfulness to the semantic tenor with as little interference as possible from the constraints of the vehicle" (Johnson, Barbara. "Taking Fidelity Philosophically." *Difference in Translation,* ed. Joseph F. Graham. Cornell

University Press, 1985). But difficulties arise when the constitutive "constraint" of the vehicle—namely, the rhetoricity of the linguistic medium—threatens to interfere with the reliable production of meaning, and so with understanding. If to understand a text entails first of all a determination of its referential mode, the problematics of translation return James's reader to the question of reference posed by the "portrait" that is, according to its author, "not a portrait." In the terms of James's figure for criticism—the "happy portrait" that is "really . . . a text preserved by translation"—what is at issue is a temporally complex relation between languages, and not the mimetic relation of a visual representation to an external referent. If the portrait can yet be said (rightly or wrongly) to refer, the reference in question is of the order of the translation's "reference" to its original—that is, a reference whose assured success cannot be taken for granted. The threat posed to successful reference (to the "happiness" of the portrait) is a function of the tension between figuration (e.g. the metaphorics of translation and original) and meaning. Such a tension structures the chapter, singled out by James as exemplary, in which Isabel turns reader to undertake her "vigil of searching criticism."

"SHE HAD NOT READ HIM RIGHT."

From the novel's outset, Isabel, like most readers, naively takes for granted the possibility of successfully determining reference, with a faith in intelligibility that extends as well to figures of speech. She operates on the assumption that tropes can be retranslated into their proper referents, so long as one can tell the literal from the figurative senses. A radical undermining of this confidence takes place during Isabel's wakeful night in the Palazzo Roccanera. The crisis recorded in chapter 42 of *The Portrait of a Lady* is a crisis of reading, and the terms of its narration are in keeping with its character as such.

The "critical hours" of Isabel's vigil begin when Osmond's words "put the situation before her," providing "the start that accompanies unexpected recognition." The situation in question is that of the deep mistrust that has become "the clearest result of their short married life"—a mutual suspicion figured as "a gulf [that] had opened between them over which they looked at each other with eyes that were on either side a declaration of the deception suffered." The progression of that mistrust is then rendered more elaborately as a gradual darkening, which proves alarming by the close of their first year together:

> Then the shadows had begun to gather; it was as if Osmond
> deliberately, almost malignantly, had put the lights out one by

one. The dusk at first was vague and thin, and she could still see her way in it. But it steadily deepened, and if now and again it occasionally lifted there were certain corners of her prospect that were impenetrably black. These shadows were not an emanation from her own mind. . . . They were a part, they were a kind of creation and consequence, of her husband's very presence.

Isabel's sense of the deepening darkness brought about by a deliberate smothering of the light as sinister as Othello's ironically reverses Osmond's earlier analogy for his prenuptial satisfaction (a satisfaction that is "more than theoretical") with the radiant Isabel: "It's just as when one has been trying to spell out a book in the twilight and suddenly the lamp comes in. I had been putting out my eyes over the book of life and finding nothing to reward me for my pains; but now that I can read it properly I see it's a delightful story." Osmond's figure and his misplaced confidence in his own "proper" reading anticipate the reading Isabel undertakes as a result of her "unexpected recognition"—a reading of her history of reading. "Scanning the future," she is convinced that Osmond "would if possible never give her a pretext, never put himself in the wrong," and that she on the other hand, despite her best efforts, "would give him many pretexts," "would often put herself in the wrong." Her anxiety about the justification she may inadvertently give her husband immediately precedes her reading of the pretext of their shared past ("preserved," like the text in translation, in the pluperfect of her narrated recollection), and in particular of the unintentional but "complete" deception to which both have been subject:

She had effaced herself when he first knew her; she had made herself small, pretending there was less of her than there really was. . . . He was not changed, he had not disguised himself, during the year of his courtship, any more than she. But she had seen only half of his nature then, as one saw the disk of the moon when it was partly masked by the shadow of the earth. She saw the full moon now—she saw the whole man. She had kept still, as it were, so that he should have a free field, and yet in spite of this she had mistaken a part for the whole.

A twofold error emerges from her recollection, in which both husband and wife are implicated: 1) Isabel sees only "half" of the partly-masked man she consents to marry; 2) she effaces herself in turn, offering to his understanding only a part in lieu of the whole. Her double deception—her mistaking (and misgiving) a part for the whole, is explicitly recollected and recounted as an error in reading, and specifically in reading the sense of the figure:

> during those months she had imagined a world of things that had no substance. She had a more wondrous vision of him, fed through charmed senses and oh such a stirred fancy!—she had not read him right. A certain combination of features had touched her, and in them she had seen the most striking of figures.

The New York edition of the novel emphatically rewrites "she had a vision of him" as "she had not read him right." The "striking" figure in question, which she "sees" but fails to read, is specifiable as synecdoche, that versatile trope whereby "a more comprehensive term is used for a less comprehensive or vice versa; as whole for part or part for whole, genus for species or species for genus, etc." (*OED*). As such, it is the figure, for example, that enables James, in his preface, to speak of Isabel's vigil as "a supreme illustration of the general plan"—i.e. as a part that can stand in for the whole. It allows him as well to anticipate Isabel's error, and to offer an excuse in advance when he acknowledges, in the notebook entry on *The Portrait,* the "obvious criticism" that it leaves the heroine hanging: "The whole of anything is never told; you can only take what groups together. What I have done has that unity—it groups together."

In its articulation of part and whole, and its assumption of a continuity, of an organic coherence between the two, synecdoche is closely allied to another, more familiar rhetorical term. In Coleridge's landmark formulation in *The Statesman's Manual,* synecdoche provides the structure of the symbol, which, in contrast to "unsubstantial" allegory, "always partakes of the Reality which it renders intelligible; and while it enunciates the whole, abides itself as a living part in that Unity, of which it is the representative." In these terms, which have in great measure dictated the Romantic and post-Romantic understanding of this figure, the symbol affords the possibility of a coincidence between representative "image" and "substance," which are related as part to whole. This possibility in turn enables Isabel's misreading, which entails precisely looking for "substance" where there is only image ("she had imagined a world of things that had no substance"). More specifically, she identifies the part with the (partly masked) whole— that is, forgets the substitution on which the "striking figure" is founded, and the difference such a substitution necessarily introduces. If "she had not read him right," it is because she (mis)takes the figure literally, "translates" it faithfully, *verbum pro verbo,* thus bearing out Madame Merle's accusation that she is "too literal." (One could also argue, given the text's characterization of Osmond as "pure form," that Isabel confuses the formal and semantic properties of language.) The motivation for doing so—consistent with that specified by the rhetoricians for the use of synecdoche— is the broader and deeper meaning she wants to read into Osmond, whom Ralph, Mrs. Touchett and others recognize as "narrow" and "shallow." She takes the partial figure for the totality of a meaning that proves mistaken, unreliable. Her choice of Osmond, "translated" into the terminology of reading, figures a choice of meaning at the expense of rhetoric, a falsely referential translation of the figure—a "forgetting" of the figurality of language for the sake of the illusion that it can properly and unproblematically mean. When Isabel asks herself, in the course of her nocturnal reflections, "if she had really married on a factitious theory," she has in mind a "theory" about the role of her inheritance, and of Osmond's suitability as a charitable institution, in her decision to wed; and she is able to answer readily that "this was only half the story." Her recognition during her critical vigil is that the meaning she has grasped is only partial, that she has failed to comprehend "the whole thing"—that if she married on a theory of her own contriving, it was well a theory of reading that forgot the complexities introduced by figuration.

A possible "motive" for Isabel's literalization of synecdoche is theorized otherwise in Kenneth Burke's account of the figure in *A Grammar of Motives,* where it numbers (along with metaphor, metonymy and irony) among the four "master tropes." Burke's primary concern, like Isabel's, is not with its "purely figurative usage," but with synecdoche's "role in the discovery and description of 'the truth'." After noting the instability of "the dividing line between the figurative and literal usages," Burke substitutes for the name of the trope his own name for its " 'literal' or 'realistic' application"; by way of this exchange, synecdoche (understood "in the usual range of dictionary sense, with such meanings as: part for the whole, whole for the part, container for the contained, sign for the thing signified, material for the thing made . . . cause for effect, effect for cause, genus for species, species for genus, etc." becomes "representation." In the Burkean scheme, "any act of representation automatically implies a synecdochic relationship," and the synecdochic conversion in turn implies "an integral relationship, a relationship of convertibility, between the two terms." The model for the theory is political representation, "where some part of the social body (either traditionally established, or elected, or coming into authority by revolution) is held to be 'representative' of the society as a whole." (The political basis of the " 'realistic' application" of synecdoche is thematized in the debate about English politics early in the novel itself, chiefly among the Tory Touchetts and Warburton, a radical reformer.) Representation in Burke's sense is thus allied with the "reduction" of metonymy: "If I reduce the contours of the United States, for instance, to the terms of a relief map, I have within these limits 'represented' the U. S. . . . Thus . . . reduction/metonymy . . . overlaps upon synecdoche." Burke's example is itself figured in the novel in the person of Henrietta Stackpole, who according to Isabel is

> "a kind of emanation of the great democracy—of the continent, the country, the nation. I don't say that she sums it all up, that would be too much to ask of her. But she suggests it; she vividly figures it. . . . Henrietta presents herself, and I'm straightway convinced by *her*; not so much in respect to herself as in respect to what masses behind her."
>
> "Ah, you mean the back view of her," Ralph suggested.
>
> "What she says is true," his cousin answered; "you'll never be serious. I like the great country stretching away beyond the rivers and across the prairies. . . . A strong, sweet, fresh odour seems to rise from it, and Henrietta—pardon my simile—has something of that odour in her garments."

Isabel's apologetic effort to figure Henrietta's representative status is her literalized by Ralph Touchett, who is finally persuaded to acknowledge Isabel's "imagination" and to agree that "Henrietta does smell of the future—it almost knocks one down!" (Cf. Poirier's reading of the passage: "The possibility of a human being representing something or someone else, which bears . . . on what happens eventually to Isabel . . . is here the object of comic ridicule. Henrietta becomes in Isabel's description a grossly literal representation of the size and smell of the whole American continent." But it is rather in Ralph's reading than in Isabel's figuring that the literalization takes place.)

Graver is the context in which Ralph's later reflection "reduces" Isabel to a "representation" of her husband:

> Her light step drew a majesty of drapery behind it; her intelligent head sustained a majesty of ornament. The free, keen girl had become quite another person; what he saw was the fine lady who was supposed to represent something. What did Isabel represent? Ralph asked himself; and he could only answer by saying that she represented Gilbert Osmond.

"Representation," in this context, does not resolve itself into a structure of part and whole. Its sense here is opposed by Ralph to that of another term, "expression," which arises in the context of his frustration at Isabel's determined dissimulation of her "real situation," her marital misery: "for him she would always wear a mask . . . if she wore a mask it completely covered her face. There was something fixed and mechanical in the serenity painted on it; this was not an expression, Ralph said—it was a representation, it was even an advertisement." The term "expression" is itself debated earlier in the narrative, in the context of a disagreement between Isabel and Madame Merle about modes of self-expression in particular. Madame Merle argues that "One's self—for other people—is one's expression of one's self; and one's house, one's furniture, one's garments, the books one reads, the company one keeps—these things are all expressive"; Isabel is not persuaded, and offers a different view:

> I think just the other way. I don't know whether I succeed in expressing myself, but I know that nothing else expresses me. Nothing that belongs to me is any measure of me; everything's on the contrary a limit, a barrier, and a perfectly arbitrary one. Certainly the clothes which, as you say, I choose to wear, don't express me; and heaven forbid they should! . . . To begin with it's not my choice that I wear them; they are imposed on me by society.

Isabel's early recognition of the limited, arbitrary and imposed character of expression returns to her in the course of her meditative vigil, her recollection of moments when she was less adept as a reader.

Neither, in the sense in which Ralph understands it, does "representation" express what it is supposed to represent—it rather "masks" it, dissimulates it—in short upsets the symmetry of the synecdochic exchange (whereby, for Burke, "As a mental state is the 'representation' of certain material conditions, so we could—reversing the process—say that the material conditions are 'representative' of the mental state."). For the reader of *The Portrait,* the question of "representation" (like the question of the "portrait") becomes a version of an inquiry entailed in Ralph's early attempt to decipher one of the inscrutable telegrams composed by his mother: "In what sense is the term used?"

To consider (let alone to answer) such a question, as its posing in the novel's first chapter attests, is to weigh a multiplicity of further questions that also prove finally to be questions of reading. Ralph recites the contents of his mother's opaque text and their perplexed response:

" 'Changed hotel, very bad, impudent clerk, address here. Taken sister's girl, died last year, go to Europe, two sisters, quite independent.' Over that my father and I have scarcely stopped puzzling; it seems to admit of so many interpretations. . . . We thought at first that the sister mentioned might be the sister of the clerk; but the subsequent mention of a niece seems to prove that the allusion is to one of my aunts. Then there was a question as to whose the two other sisters were; they are probably two of my late aunt's daughters. But who's 'quite independent,' and in what sense is the term used?—that point's not yet settled. Does the expression apply more particulary to the young lady my mother had adopted, or does it characterise her sisters equally?—and is it used in a moral or in a financial sense? Does it mean that they've been left well off, or that they wish to be under no obligations? or does it simply mean that they're fond of their own way? . . . We're quite in the dark."

The darkness in which Ralph and his father find themselves as they attempt to decipher Mrs. Touchett's enigmatic missive pales by comparison with the shadows (like the shadow of the earth that "partly masked the disk of the moon" in Isabel's simile for her error in reading Osmond, her figure for the text's figure of synecdoche) that have gathered around Isabel by the time of her vigil in "the house of darkness, the house of dumbness, the house of suffocation." Both "situations," nonetheless, call for a reading, which the novel frames as a choice among options. (As Paul de Man argues,

> Any reading always involves a choice between signification and symbolization, and this choice can be made only if one postulates the possibility of distinguishing the literal from the figural. This decision is not arbitrary, since it is based on a variety of textual and contextual factors [grammar, lexicology, tradition, usage, tone, declarative statement, diacritical marks, etc.]. But the necessity of making such a decision cannot be avoided or the entire order of discourse would collapse. The situation implies that figural discourse is always understood in contradistinction to a form of discourse that would not be figural; it postulates, in other words, the possibility of referential meaning as the *telos* of all language. It would be quite foolish to assume that one can lightheartedly move away from the constraint of referential meaning.

> [*Allegories of Reading*]

Isabel's attempt to move away from the constraint of Osmond's "rigid system," her increasingly desperate "resistance" [the resistance of the original to translation], is enacted with a heavy heart indeed.) Isabel's initial decision to marry Osmond—retrospectively read in chapter 42—and her more problematic determination to return to him at the novel's conclusion, must be understood, then, in light of the complex choices entailed in reading.

The Portrait's RHETORIC OF TEMPORALITY

The temporality of Isabel's critical vigil, recounted in the pluperfect of retrospect, is dictated in part by the narrator's decision to interrupt the sequence of events to vault over the first year of the Osmonds' married life, which falls between the closing line of chapter 35 and the opening of 36. Nonetheless, as Dorrit Cohn remarks, "the function of Isabel's flashback is not primarily to fill this gap; her remembering psyche does not focus on the elided events themselves, but engages in a kind of retrospective self-analysis." Notable as well is a lapse from the pluperfect in the narrative, following Isabel's realization of her error, in a passage that affords an analogy for her former misunderstanding of Osmond, and with it "a new grammatical dimension, and new semantic complications":

> She felt at the time that he was helpless and ineffectual, but the feeling had taken the form of a tenderness which was the very flower of respect. He was like a sceptical voyager strolling on the beach while he waited for the tide, looking seaward yet not putting to sea. She would launch his boat for him; she would be his providence; it would be a good thing to love him. And she had loved him, she had so anxiously and yet so ardently given herself.

As Cohn observes, the conditional tense of the sentence beginning "She would launch his boat . . . " "can only be a narrated monologue of Isabel's past illusions about the future: a future that, at the moment of her retrospection, already lies in her disillusioned past." Moreover, the passage is further complicated, for "the preceding sentence in simple past ('He was like a skeptical voyager . . . ') which on first reading looked like a lapsed pluperfect, can now be interpreted with equal validity as a narrated monologue to the second degree, nested within the narrated memory."

The "second degree" temporal complexities subtly traced by Cohn—the past projection of a future itself now past—characterize a chapter that might be argued to divide The Portrait in two with respect to its heroine's self-understanding: that is, into a mystified condition that precedes it, and a state that, thanks to the "vigil of searching criticism," has recovered from the delusion it now recognizes as such. But one would be "both right and wrong" to read Isabel's *metanoia* in chapter 42 in terms of successive stages of consciousness, as one would be to read her simply as a portrait of Minny Temple, though the errors are of a different order. To avoid retranslating the textual terms of the present analysis back into the phenomenological vocabulary of the experience of a consciousness (and the double bind that would entail), the reader must articulate the temporality of the narrative with the rhetorical structure that, in the instance of chapter 42 of *The Portrait,* is an operative as well as a thematic construct: namely, the structure of synecdoche, of the symbol.

If prior to her marriage and during its first benighted months Isabel had "mistaken a part for the whole," had "imagined a world of things that had no substance," her error is explicable, even excusable, in rhetorical terms. The structure of synecdoche promises, with its intersubstitution of part and whole, the coincidence of "image" and "substance," since part and whole do not differ in kind, but only in extension. In temporal terms, moreover, the synecdochic/symbolic relation is one of simultaneity; the intervention of time proves merely contingent in what is finally a spatial model. It is here that *The Portrait,* most apparently in its self-division into a "before" and an "after" in chapter 42, exceeds the categories of part and whole, and requires a rhetorical analysis that is not confined to the simultaneity of the synecdoche (or of metaphor or any such substitutive trope), but that can provide for a text whose temporality is crucial and complicated. A pivotal term for such an analysis is provided in the novel, in a passage that ironically prefigures Isabel's misreading. The passage begins with Ralph Touchett's pluperfect memory of Isabel's early insistence on her fondness for her freedom:

> She had wanted to see life, and fortune was serving her to her taste; a succession of fine gentlemen going down on their knees to her would do as well as anything else. Ralph looked forward to a fourth, a fifth, a tenth besieger; he had no conviction she would stop at a third. She would keep the gate ajar and open a parley; she would certainly not allow number three to come in. He expressed this view, somewhat after this fashion, to his mother, who looked at him as if he had been dancing a jig. He had such a fanciful, pictorial way of saying things that he might as well address her in the deaf-mute's alphabet.

Ralph's densely figured recollection projects backward to embrace Isabel's earlier formulation of her desire, and forward to his own version of her future. Mrs. Touchett is characteristically impatient with such complexity, and responds: " 'I don't think I know what you mean,' she said; 'you use too many figures of speech; I could never understand allegories. The two words in the language I most respect are Yes and No. If Isabel wants to marry Mr. Osmond she'll do so in spite of all your comparisons.' " In one sense, the course of events proves his mother right—Isabel indeed marries despite Ralph's vested interest and his metaphors. On the other hand, Mrs. Touchett's binary logic cannot admit the disruptive force of rhetoric, and fails to comprehend the allegorical dimension of the text of Isabel's past and future—a failure that James's reader cannot afford to repeat. The narrative of Isabel's demystification in chapter 42 unfolds a temporal predicament, a temporal destiny that is readable as an allegory. If the structure of synecdoche posits a unity, an identity of part (here, image) and whole (substance), allegory on the other hand marks the "gulf," the difference that divides the present from a prior moment.

Isabel's night thoughts take the past as their "pretext" and make it newly legible by way of critical reflection, which brings with it the dawning of an awareness that dispels the figurative darkness in which she has found herself. The critical vigil comes to terms with the figure (synecdoche) whose misreading led to error, but the narrative that this coming-to-terms itself engenders—an allegory of the figure and its misreading—casts the shadow of a radical indeterminacy over the past as well as the future. Isabel, in other words, does not—cannot—learn her lesson once and for all. Intelligent and flexible of mind, she seems at moments equal to the complex double process or reading required by allegory: for instance in the awkward meeting preceding Lord Warburton's final departure from Rome, which takes place in the shadow of Osmond's frustrated hopes for his daughter's marriage to the nobleman:

> A complex operation, as she sat there, went on in her mind. On one side she listened to their visitor; said what was proper to him: read, more or less, between the lines of what he said himself; and wondered how he would have spoken if he had found her alone. On the other side she had a perfect consciousness of Osmond's emotion.

While she is thus a skilled reader-between-the-lines, the case of allegory, as Ralph notes earlier in another context, proves "an anomaly which for the moment challenged all [her] ingenuity of interpretation. To read between the lines was easier than to follow the text." Isabel's detour from the text (much as she would resist the comparison) is a version of Mrs. Touchett's impatience with "figures of speech," her inability, in particular, to "understand allegories," how they mean and fail to mean.

In the exchange between Ralph Touchett and his mother, his allegorical scenario for Isabel's future (which takes the form of a procession of rejected suitors) has the communicative effectiveness of an address "in the deaf-mute's alphabet"—that is, in a system comprised of alternately mimetic ("pictorial") and arbitrary ("fanciful") signs that substitute for speech, designed for and decipherable by the handicapped reader: in other words, a sign system that is not based on a single mode of reference, but that incorporates alternative possibilities. Likewise, the relationship between the allegorical sign and its meaning is not decided in advance; indeed, what counts for purposes of reading allegory is rather the relationship between the sign and another sign. Missing from this alphabet, an otherwise resonant figure for the complex referential mode of allegory, is the constitutive temporal dimension, for the function of the allegorical sign is to refer to another sign that is anterior to it, with which it cannot hope ever to coincide. Though the temporal disjunction it thus entails precludes the coincidence of image and substance promised by the figure of synecdoche, allegory can be "translated" into referential terms. Indeed, it requires reference, though not of the order of the mimetic reference of the "portrait" to a model, which posits a coincidence of fiction and the *hors-texte*. It would be more accurate to say that the reference of the allegorical sign to its antecedent is "like" the reference—problematic as that is—of a translation to the prior text it "preserves."

The disjunction between the allegorical sign and the antecedent to which it thus "refers" is figured in the well-known passage in chapter 28, in which Isabel contemplates the Greek sculpture that has been "translated" to the gallery of the Capitol in Rome:

> She sat down in the circle of these presences, regarding them vaguely, resting her eyes on their beautiful blank faces; listening, as it were, to their eternal silence. It is impossible, in Rome at least, to look long at a great company of Greek sculptures without feeling the effect of their noble quietude . . . the deep stillness of the past, so vivid yet, though it is nothing but a void full of names, seems to throw a solemn spell upon them. . . . Isabel sat there a long time, under the charm of their motionless grace, wondering to what, of their experience, their absent eyes were open, and how, to our ears, their alien lips would sound. . . . She had seen them all before, but her enjoyment repeated itself.

The pastness of the past as imaged in the "shining antique marbles" prompts

Isabel to wonder "how, to our ears," the alien tongue of the deaf-mute statues might sound—whether their silent speech might be translated out of the "void" of the past (a void full of untranslatable proper names) into a language we could understand, could read. Like the ill-fated Atlantic crossing of the English idiom narrated in "The Question of Our Speech," by which "our medium of utterance was to be disjoined from all the associations, the other presences, that had attended her," Isabel's speculative translation of the statues' alien language argues a disjunction from the past (which is figured as "blank," "eternally silent," "still," and above all "absent"), a disarticulation of its sense. Isabel does not read in this scene—she "sees" the statues, as she has "seen them all before." The allusion to repetition—here a pleasurable reprise of aesthetic appreciation—also signals the repetition (with a difference) by the allegorical sign of its antecedent; moreover, it prefigures, in a way characteristic of the mode, the future repetition of the past error of reading to which Isabel seems inescapably fated. Despite her recognition, during the critical vigil narrated in chapter 42, both of her mistake in identifying the part with the whole—literalizing the synecdoche—and of its cost, Isabel's final decision to return to Osmond is readable as a repetition of her former interpretive error. The "figure" (like that of the "overmuffled" princess of "one of the ages of dress" that images Rome for Isabel) "drag[s] a train" behind it—in this case, the allegorical train of unreadability and its attendant misreadings.

The novel's final chapter, in which Isabel turns a deaf ear to the reasoned advice of her friends and departs for Rome and Osmond, must thus be understood in the light of the scene of reading staged in chapter 42, to which it indeed "refers" along allegorical lines. Chapter 55 opens at Gardencourt, where her adventure commenced, and where she has returned for a last meeting with Ralph. Following his death, she learns of Ralph's bequest of his library to Henrietta "in recognition of her services to literature." Isabel herself, the narrator reports, "had never been less interested in literature than today, as she found when she occasionally took down from the shelf one of the rare and valuable volumes of which Mrs. Touchett had spoken. She was quite unable to read; her attention had never been so little at her command." Her inability to read establishes the framework for the final interview—and struggle—with Caspar Goodwood, who pleads with her to circumscribe the error and pain of the past: "You must save what you can of your life; you musn't lose it all simply because you've lost a part." In urging her to free herself from Osmond, Caspar distinguishes the elements of synecdoche, and asks her not to sacrifice the whole by subsuming it in the part. The figure that structures her retrospective vigil proves crucial once more: when he insistently asks "Why should you go back—why should you go through that ghastly form?" her reply ("To get away from you!") "expressed only a little of what she felt. The rest was that she had never been loved before. She had believed it, but this was different." In this instance of difference, the parts (the "little of what she felt" and "the rest") fail to constitute a coherent whole, and the resulting "confusion" makes Isabel's head "swim." Thereupon follows the infamous narration of the lightning kiss: "and it was extraordinarily as if, while she took it, she felt each thing in his hard manhood that had least pleased her, each aggressive fact of his face, his figure, his presence, justified of its intense identity and made one with this act of possession." The "extraordinarily *as if*" signals the figural mode in which Isabel "felt" the component parts of his "manhood" "made one"—totalized into a whole. What is "confused" about the identification of the parts that takes place here is expressed in the rather opaque sentence immediately following: "So had she heard of those wrecked and under water following a train of images before they sink." The train of images, the figures in the allegorical procession, cannot be halted, closed off with a totalizing reading like the one that identifies the part with the whole.

When the lightning fades and the darkness returns,

> she was free. She never looked about her; she only darted from the spot. . . . In an extraordinarily short time—for the distance was considerable—she had moved through the darkness (for she saw nothing) and reached the door. . . . She had not known where to turn, but she knew now. There was a very straight path.

The swift forward movement in the darkness, a citation of her early formula for freedom, in fact propels her along a very straight path back to Rome and the bondage of a miserable marriage. How, then, is Isabel's perverse insistence on returning to Osmond—her sacrifice of the whole with the part—explicable? If she continues to pay for a past error (the misreading of the "figure") whose consequences (or "train") cannot be circumscribed, and whose future repetition cannot be averted, what are the terms of payment?

To judge by most critics of *The Portrait*, the terms are first and finally ethical. According to the simplest outline of an interpretation that has many variants, Isabel takes her vow of marriage to Osmond, as well as her promise not to abandon her stepdaughter, seriously, indeed literally. She sacrifices her own freedom, her own future, for the sake of a bond which, as she reflects during the vigil, "there was more . . . than she had meant to put her name to." Poirier, for example, writes of the "very painful moral scrupulousness" that marks James's relation not only to Isabel Archer, but to all his characters: "He was terribly afraid of denying to any of them the fullest opportunity for self-dramatization, of limiting their freedom of expression by defining them too categorically. And yet it need hardly be said that he is given to categorizations and to definitions of character which are close to the allegorical." The burden of reading *The Portrait of a Lady,* in this light, is to articulate the novel's "moral scrupulousness" with its allegorical mode—to reconcile the problematizing (temporally) of reference and (rhetorically) of meaning entailed in allegory with the novel's moral tone and thematics.

The temptation to which many interpreters of the novel have yielded is, in the instance of Isabel's decision to return to Osmond, to sacrifice allegory to moral scrupulousness, and to read the passage in strictly thematic terms—to give, that is, a referential version of what is arguably a linguistic predicament. One might counter this canonical view with the assertion that it is allegory's temporal disjunction and rhetorical disarticulation that are thematized in Isabel's perplexing act of renunciation. The latter reading makes possible an account of the novel's ethical framework that does not simply appeal to thematic categories like agency and free will; indeed, it redefines the novel's moral imperatives in linguistic rather than subjective terms. *The Portrait's* complex ethicity thus becomes readable as the referential staging of a rhetorical dilemma.

The linguistic "confusion" that frames Isabel's fateful decision is arguably a function of her short memory. (Blackmur writes of Isabel's fate that "What will happen to her haunts us like a memory we cannot quite reenact." It is perhaps a question as well of a memory Isabel herself can *only* reenact, has no choice *but* to reenact.) Not only does she forget the specific lesson of her critical vigil—do not mistake the part for the whole—and thus condemn herself to repeating her earlier error. She also forgets, habitually, about the past in general:

> It was in her disposition at all times to lose faith in the reality of absent things; she could summon back her faith, in case of need, with an effort, but the effort was often painful even when the reality had been pleasant. The past was apt to look dead and its revival rather to show the livid light of a judgement day. . . . She was capable of being wounded by the discovery that she had been forgotten; but of all liberties the one she herself found sweetest was the liberty to forget.

Freedom for Isabel is above all freedom to forget—which she is disposed to do "at all times," not excepting her moments of acute retrospection during the critical vigil in chapter 42. The forgetting here has a specific object: "She heard the small hours strike, and then the great ones, but her vigil took no heed of time. Her mind, assailed by visions, was in a state of extraordinary activity, and her visions might as well come to her there, where she sat up to meet them, as on her pillow, to make a mockery of rest." Not to take heed of time (or to take heed of it, in the mode of Mrs. Touchett, only as clock-time, as the register of the present, as when Isabel "read all this as she would have read the hour on the clock-face") is to be unable to read the past, to "preserve" it, translate it into a future that would be something other than the repetition of a past error.

It is perhaps the possibility of such a future that Isabel seeks to read in the absent eyes and alien lips of the antique marbles in the Roman Capitol—a possibility to which Walter Benjamin, like James, gives form and figure:

> Torso. Nur wer die eigene Vergangenheit als Ausgeburt des Zwanges und der Not zu betrachten wuesste, der waere faehig, sie in jeder Gegenwart aufs hoechste fuer sich wert zu machen. Denn was einer lebte, ist bestenfalls der schoenen Figur vergleichbar, der auf Transporten alle Glieder abgeschlagen wurden, und die nun nichts als den kostbaren Block abgibt, aus dem er das Bild seiner Zukunft zu hauen hat.
>
> (*Einbahnstrasse*)

> ("Torso.—Only he knows to view his own past as an abortion sprung from compulsion and need can use it to full advantage in the present. For what one has lived is at best comparable to the beautiful statue [*Figur*] which has had all its limbs knocked off in transit, and now yields nothing but the precious block out of which the image [*Bild*] of its future must be hewn.")

If these figures for the past have been knocked about in transit, have lost something in translation, the same may be said of *The Portrait*, which has suffered an analogous amputation at the hands of critics forgetful of its temporal and rhetorical complexity. James's novel nonetheless continues to yield (nothing but) the text out of which the "portrait" of its critical future must be rendered.

Chronology

1843	Henry James born on April 15 in New York City.
1843–45	James family travels to Europe.
1845–55	Lives in New York City and Albany.
1855–58	Lives in Europe, attending schools in Geneva, London, Paris, and Boulogne.
1858	Spends summer in Newport, Rhode Island.
1859	Visits Europe.
1860–62	Returns to Newport.
1862–63	Enrolled at Harvard Law School.
1864	Publishes first story, "A Tragedy of Error."
1869–70	First trip to Europe alone, during which he hears of his cousin Minny Temple's death.
1871	*Watch and Ward* published serially in the *Atlantic Monthly*.
1872–74	Trip to Europe with sister Alice.
1875	*A Passionate Pilgrim* and *Transatlantic Sketches* published; *Roderick Hudson* appears serially in the *Atlantic Monthly*.
1876	Goes to Paris for extended stay, but moves to London in disaffection with Paris life.
1877	*The American.*
1878	*French Poets and Novelists, The Europeans,* and *Daisy Miller.*
1879	*Hawthorne.*
1880	*Confidence* and *Washington Square.*
1881	*The Portrait of a Lady.* Returns to New York for short stay.
1882	Returns to U.S. once more after death of Henry James, Sr.
1883	Returns to London; *The Siege of London* and *Portraits of Places.*
1884	*A Little Tour in France* and *Tales of Three Cities.*
1885	*The Author of "Beltraffio," The Bostonians,* and *The Princess Casamassima.*

1888   *Partial Portraits.*

1890   *The Tragic Muse;* starts writing for the stage (dramatic versions of *The American, Disengaged, Guy Domville*).

1895   Returns to writing novels and short stories on the failure of *Guy Domville;* publishes *The Other House* and *Embarrassments.*

1897   *The Spoils of Poynton* and *What Maisie Knew.*

1898   *The Turn of the Screw* and *In the Cage;* moves to Lamb House at Rye.

1899   *The Awkward Age.*

1901   *The Sacred Fount.*

1902   *The Wings of the Dove.*

1903   *The Ambassadors* and *William Wetmore Story and His Friends.*

1904   *The Golden Bowl;* sets out on a year-long tour of his native country, which forms the basis for *The American Scene* (1907).

1906   Returns to England; revises early work and writes prefaces for the New York edition of his works (1907).

1908   Play, *The High Bid,* produced in Edinburgh.

1909   Unable to work on account of nervous illness.

1913   *A Small Boy and Others.*

1914   *Notes of a Son and Brother* and *Notes on Novelists.* Embarks on civilian war work at the outbreak of World War I in Europe, while writing *The Ivory Tower,* which is left unfinished. Starts work on *The Sense of the Past,* also left unfinished.

1915   Obtains British citizenship.

1916   Dies of a stroke, February 28.

Contributors

HAROLD BLOOM, Sterling Professor of the Humanities at Yale University, is the author of *The Anxiety of Influence, Poetry and Repression,* and many other volumes of literary criticism. His forthcoming study, *Freud: Transference and Authority,* attempts a full-scale reading of all of Freud's major writings. A MacArthur Prize Fellow, he is the general editor of five series of literary criticism published by Chelsea House.

RICHARD POIRIER, Professor of English at Rutgers University, is editor-in-chief of *Raritan* and an editor of the Library of America series. His many publications include *Norman Mailer, The Performing Self, A World Elsewhere,* and *Robert Frost.*

LAURENCE BEDWELL HOLLAND was Professor of English and American Literature at Johns Hopkins University. He was the editor of *Design in America* and the author of *The Expense of Vision: Essays on the Craft of Henry James.*

NINA BAYM is Professor of English at the University of Illinois at Urbana. She is the author of *The Shape of Hawthorne's Career* and has written on Cooper, Melville, James, and on women's fiction.

ELIZABETH ALLEN is the author of *A Woman's Place in the Novels of Henry James.*

DAVID M. LUBIN teaches Art History at Colby College. He is the author of *Act of Portrayal: Eakins, Sargent, James.*

MARIA IRENE RAMALHO DE SOUSA SANTOS is Chairman of the Department of Comparative Literature and Professor of American Studies at the University of Coimbra, Portugal. She has written on Wallace Stevens and Henry James and on modern Portuguese poetry.

DEBORAH ESCH is Assistant Professor of English at Princeton University and is the author of a forthcoming book on James.

Bibliography

Agnew, Jean-Christophe. "The Consuming Vision of Henry James." In *The Culture of Consumption: Critical Essays in American History, 1880–1980,* edited by Richard Wightman Fox and T. J. Jackson Lears, 67–100. New York: Pantheon, 1983.

Allott, Miriam. "Form versus Substance in Henry James." *The Review of English Literature* 3, no. 1 (1962): 53–66.

Anderson, Charles. *Person, Place, and Thing in Henry James's Novels.* Durham, N.C.: Duke University Press, 1977.

Anderson, Quentin. *The American Henry James.* New Brunswick, N.J.: Rutgers University Press, 1957.

Andreas, Osborne. *Henry James and the Expanding Horizon: A Study of Meaning and Basic Themes of James's Fiction.* Seattle: University of Washington Press, 1948.

Auchincloss, Louis. *Reading Henry James.* Minneapolis: University of Minnesota Press, 1975.

Banta, Martha. *Henry James and the Occult: The Great Extension.* Bloomington: Indiana University Press, 1972.

Beach, Joseph Warren. *The Method of Henry James.* Rev. ed. Philadelphia: Albert Saifer, 1954.

Berland, Alwyn. *Culture and Conduct in the Novels of Henry James.* Cambridge: Cambridge University Press, 1981.

Bewley, Marius. *The Complex Fate.* London: Chatto & Windus, 1952.

Blackmur, R. P. *Studies in Henry James.* New York: New Directions, 1983.

Booth, Bradford A. "Henry James and the Economic Motif." *Nineteenth-Century Fiction* 8 (September 1953): 141–50.

Bowden, Edwin T. *The Themes of Henry James: A System of Observation through the Visual Arts.* New Haven, Conn.: Yale University Press, 1956.

Brooks, Van Wyck. *The Pilgrimage of Henry James.* New York: Dutton, 1925.

Buitenhuis, Peter. *The Grasping Imagination: The American Writings of Henry James.* Toronto: University of Toronto Press, 1970.

———, ed. *Twentieth-Century Interpretations of* The Portrait of a Lady: *A Collection of Critical Essays.* Englewood Cliffs, N.J.: Prentice-Hall, 1968.

Cargill, Oscar. *The Novels of Henry James.* New York: Macmillan, 1961.

Chase, Richard. *The American Novel and Its Traditions.* Garden City, N.Y.: Doubleday, 1957.

Clair, John A. *The Ironic Dimension in the Fiction of Henry James*. Pittsburgh: Duquesne University Press, 1965.

Cohn, Dorrit. *Transparent Minds: Narrative Modes for Presenting Consciousness in Fiction*. Princeton: Princeton University Press, 1978.

Collins, Martha. "Narrator, the Satellites, and Isabel Archer: Point of View in *The Portrait of a Lady*." *Studies in the Novel* 8 (1976): 142–56.

Crews, Frederick C. *The Tragedy of Manners*. New Haven, Conn.: Yale University Press, 1957.

Donadio, Stephen. *Nietzsche, Henry James, and the Artistic Will*. New York: Oxford University Press, 1978.

Dupee, F. W. *Henry James*. New York: Sloane, 1951.

Edel, Leon. *Henry James*. 5 vols. Philadelphia: Lippincott, 1953–72.

———, ed. *Henry James: A Collection of Critical Essays*. Englewood Cliffs, N.J.: Prentice-Hall, 1963.

Feidelson, Charles. "The Moment of *Portrait of a Lady*." *Ventures* 8, no. 2 (Fall 1968): 47–55.

Felman, Shoshana. "Turning the Screw of Interpretation." *Yale French Studies* 55/56 (1977): 94–207.

Fogel, Daniel Mark. *Henry James and the Structure of the Romantic Imagination*. Baton Rouge: Louisiana State University Press, 1981.

Fowler, Virginia C. *Henry James's American Girl: The Embroidery on the Canvas*. Madison: University of Wisconsin Press, 1984.

Gale, Robert L. *The Caught Image: Figurative Language in the Fiction of Henry James*. Chapel Hill: University of North Carolina Press, 1964.

Gard, Roger, ed. *Henry James: The Critical Heritage*. London: Routledge & Kegan Paul, 1968.

Goode, John, ed. *The Air of Reality: New Essays on Henry James*. London: Methuen, 1972.

Graham, Kenneth. *Henry James: The Drama of Fulfilment*. Oxford: Clarendon Press, Oxford University Press, 1975.

Grover, Philip. *Henry James and the French Novel: A Study in Inspiration*. New York: Barnes & Noble, 1973.

Hirsch, David H. "Henry James and the Seal of Love." *Modern Language Studies* 13, no. 4 (1983): 39–60.

Holland, Laurence Bedwell. *The Expense of Vision: Essays on the Craft of Henry James*. Princeton: Princeton University Press, 1964. Rev. ed. Baltimore: Johns Hopkins University Press, 1982.

Hutchinson, Stuart. *Henry James: American as Modernist*. New York: Barnes & Noble, 1982.

Jones, Granville H. *Henry James's Psychology of Experience: Innocence, Responsibility, and Renunciation in the Fiction of Henry James*. The Hague: Mouton, 1975.

Kappeler, Suzanne. *Writing and Reading in Henry James*. New York: Columbia University Press, 1980.

Kaston, Carren. *Imagination and Desire in the Novels of Henry James*. New Brunswick, N.J.: Rutgers University Press, 1984.

Kirsche, James J. *Henry James and Impressionism*. Troy, N.Y.: Whitson, 1981.

Krier, William. "The 'Latent Extravagance' of *The Portrait of a Lady*." *Mosaic* 9, no. 3 (1976): 57–65.

Krook, Dorothea. *The Ordeal of Consciousness in Henry James*. Cambridge: Cambridge University Press, 1962.

Labrie, Ross. "Henry James's Idea of Consciousness." *American Literature* 39 (January 1968): 517–29.

Leavis, F. R. *The Great Tradition*. New York: Stewart, 1949.

Levy, Leo B. *Versions of Melodrama*. Berkeley: University of California Press, 1965.

Leyburn, Ellen Douglas. *Strange Alloy: The Relation of Comedy to Tragedy in the Fiction of Henry James*. Chapel Hill: University of North Carolina Press, 1968.

Long, Robert Emmet. *The Great Succession: Henry James and the Legacy of Hawthorne*. Pittsburgh: University of Pittsburgh Press, 1979.

MacKenzie, Manfred. *Communities of Honor and Love in Henry James*. Cambridge: Harvard University Press, 1976.

McMaster, Juliet. "The Portrait of Isabel Archer." *American Literature* 45 (1973): 50–66.

Matthiessen, F. O. *Henry James: The Major Phase*. New York: Oxford University Press, 1963.

Mazella, Anthony J. "The New Isabel." In *The Portrait of a Lady*, edited by Robert D. Banberg. New York: Norton, 1975.

Mull, Donald K. *Henry James's "Sublime Economy."* Middletown, Conn.: Wesleyan University Press, 1973.

Norman, Ralf. *The Insecure World of Henry James's Fiction: Intensity and Ambiguity*. New York: St. Martin's, 1982.

O'Neill, John P. *Workable Design: Action and Situation in the Fiction of Henry James*. Port Washington, N.Y.: Kennikat, 1973.

Perosa, Sergio. *Henry James and the Experimental Novel*. Charlottesville: University Press of Virginia, 1978.

Poirier, Richard. *The Comic Sense of Henry James: A Study of the Early Novels*. New York: Oxford University Press, 1966.

Powers, Lyall H. *Henry James and the Naturalist Movement*. East Lansing: Michigan State University Press, 1971.

———, ed. *Henry James's Major Novels: Essays in Criticism*. East Lansing: Michigan State University Press, 1973.

Przybylowicz, Donna. *Desire and Repression: The Dialectic of Self and Other in the Late Works of Henry James*. University: University of Alabama Press, 1986.

Rahv, Philip. "Attitudes toward Henry James." In *The Question of Henry James: A Collection of Critical Essays*, edited by F. W. Dupee. New York: Holt, 1945.

Rimmon, Shlomith. *The Concept of Ambiguity—The Example of Henry James*. Chicago: University of Chicago Press, 1977.

Sabiston, Elizabeth. "The Prison of Womanhood." *Comparative Literature* 25 (1973): 336–51.

Schneider, Daniel J. *The Crystal Cage: Adventures of the Imagination in the Fiction of Henry James*. Lawrence: Regents Press of Kansas, 1978.

Sears, Sally. *The Negative Imagination: Form and Perspective in the Novels of Henry James*. Ithaca, N.Y.: Cornell University Press, 1968.

Segal, Ora. *The Lucid Reflector: The Observer in Henry James's Fiction*. New Haven, Conn.: Yale University Press, 1969.

Seltzer, Mark. *Henry James and the Art of Power*. Ithaca, N.Y.: Cornell University Press, 1984.

Sicker, Philip. *Love and the Quest for Identity in the Fiction of Henry James.* Princeton: Princeton University Press, 1980.

Stowell, Peter H. *Literary Impressionism: James and Chekhov.* Athens: University of Georgia Press, 1980.

Tanner, Tony. *Henry James I: 1843–1881.* Essex, England: Longman Group, 1979.

———, ed. *Henry James: Selections of Critical Essays.* London: Macmillan, 1968.

Van Ghent, Dorothy. *The English Novel: Form and Function.* New York: Holt, Rinehart & Winston, 1953.

Wagenknecht, Edward. *Eve and Henry James: Portraits of Women and Girls in His Fiction.* Norman: University of Oklahoma Press, 1978.

Ward, Joseph A. *The Search for Form: Studies in the Structure of James's Fiction.* Chapel Hill: University of North Carolina Press, 1967.

Weinstein, Philip M. *Henry James and the Requirements of the Imagination.* Cambridge: Harvard University Press, 1971.

Wellek, René. "Henry James's Literary Theory and Criticism." *American Literature* 30 (1958): 293–321.

Westervelt, Linda. " 'The Growing Complexity of Things': Narrative Technique in *Portrait of a Lady.*" *The Journal of Narrative Technique* 13 (1983): 74–83.

Wilson, Edmund. "The Ambiguity of Henry James." In *The Triple Thinkers,* 88–132. New York: Oxford University Press, 1963.

Winner, Viola Hopkins. *Henry James and the Visual Arts.* Charlottesville: University Press of Virginia, 1970.

Acknowledgments

"Setting the Scene: The Drama and Comedy of Judgment" (originally entitled "*The Portrait of a Lady*") by Richard Poirier from *The Comic Sense of Henry James, A Study of the Early Novels* by Richard Poirier, © 1960 by Richard Poirier. Reprinted by permission of the author and Oxford University Press.

"Organizing an Ado" (originally entitled "*The Portrait of a Lady*") by Laurence Bedwell Holland from *The Expense of Vision: Essays on the Craft of Henry James,* © 1964 by Princeton University Press. Reprinted by permission of Princeton University Press.

"Revision and Thematic Change in *The Portrait of a Lady*" by Nina Baym from *Modern Fiction Studies* 22, no. 2 (Summer 1976), © 1976 by the Purdue Research Foundation. Reprinted by permission of the Purdue Research Foundation, West Lafayette, Indiana.

"Objects of Value: Isabel and Her Inheritance" (originally entitled "*The Portrait of a Lady*") by Elizabeth Allen from *A Woman's Place in the Novels of Henry James* by Elizabeth Allen, © 1984 by Elizabeth Allen. Reprinted by permission of Macmillan Press Ltd. and St. Martin's Press, Inc.

"Act of Portrayal" (originally entitled "*The Portrait of a Lady*") by David M. Lubin from *Act of Portrayal: Eakins, Sargent, James* by David M. Lubin, © 1985 by Yale University. Reprinted by permission of Yale University Press.

"Isabel's Freedom: Henry James's *The Portrait of a Lady*" by Maria Irene Ramalho de Sousa Santos from *Biblos* 56 (1986), © 1980 by Irene Ramalho Santos. Reprinted by permission of the author.

" 'Understanding Allegories': Reading *The Portrait of a Lady*" by Deborah Esch, © 1987 by Deborah Esch. Published for the first time in this volume. Printed by permission.

Index